Garland
of
Advaitic Wisdom

Garland

of

Advaitic Wisdom

Introduction to Advaita Vedanta and
Selections of Crest Quotes from
Nondualistic Teachings

BY

ajati

sage press

PUBLISHED
BY

sage press

Daya Dharmam, R.O.A. Nagar
Tiruvannamalai – 606 603
Tamil Nadu, India

- EMAIL -
sagepressindia@yahoo.com

First Edition: August 2002

Book & Cover Design: Ajati

ISBN 81-7525-336-3

PRINTED IN INDIA

AT

ALL INDIA PRESS
P.O. Box No. 51,
Kennedy Nagar,
Pondicherry - 605 001, India

This Garland of Knowledge

is

Dedicated to the Revealer Guru

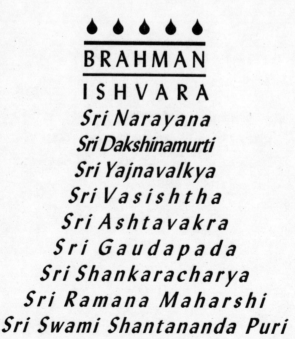

BRAHMAN

ISHVARA

Sri Narayana

Sri Dakshinamurti

Sri Yajnavalkya

Sri Vasishtha

Sri Ashtavakra

Sri Gaudapada

Sri Shankaracharya

Sri Ramana Maharshi

Sri Swami Shantananda Puri

Contents

Acknowledgements

For the development and completion of this book I received precious help from persons whom I would like to thank and give credit to.

I am indebted and would like to thank Mr. V. S. Ramanan, the President of Sri Ramanasramam, for permission to use material from books published by Sri Ramanasrarnam. My thanks go also to Mr. A. R. Natarajan, the President of the Ramana Maharshi Centre for Learning (RMCL), Bangalore, for the permission to use material from books published by RMCL.

I am profoundly grateful to my Guru, Swami Shantananda Puri Maharaj, who inspired in me fascination for and insight into Advaita Vedanta. Without his guidance, valuable expertise, and careful corrections, I am sure this book would never have been written.

Finally, I wish to thank my friends, Chris Boys, Kristin Davis, and D. Vasudevan, for their great contribution in editing and proofreading the text, and for their encouragement during the project. Thanks are also offered to Swami Devananda Saraswati who contributed his corrections and suggestions on Part One of the book.

Thanks again to all of you for the precious assistance!

ॐ

Preface

The author of *Garland of Advaitic Wisdom* – Ajati – is a fervent devotee of Sri Ramana Maharshi and an ardent advocate of Advaita Vedanta. In this book he places before the elite reader pearls of wisdom culled from various *Upanishad*-s and many other standard texts of Advaitic (non-dualistic) philosophy such as the *Ashtavakra Gita*, the *Yoga Vasishtha*, the *Ribhu Gita*, works of Sri Shankara, and the recorded teachings of Sri Ramana Maharshi. The inclusion of some sayings and stories from Zen Buddhism and Taoism, in keeping with the modern trend, lends additional color to this venture.

The underlying motif in this book is *Ajata-vada* – the doctrine of no-creation – propounded in texts like *Mandukya Karika* of Sri Gaudapada and *Ashtavakra Gita*. *Ajata-vada* holds that there has been neither creation nor dissolution, neither bondage nor release (*moksha*), neither aspirants (*sadaka*-s) to realization nor realized souls (*jnani*-s).

The introductory part gives an excellent overview of Advaita Vedanta and its proper place in Indian philosophy. It includes a concise description of the Vedanta philosophical system in general, and a more detailed accounting of the essential tenets of the Advaita School and its principal sub-schools. This first part provides the reader with the information needed to well understand and appreciate the main body of the book.

Although this is his first book in the field of Advaita, the author has been able to present an abundance of beautiful, magnificent, and relevant selections, with such perspicacity and discerning wisdom as to provide delectable verdant pastures for readers athirst for spiritual knowledge.

Hari OM !
Swami Shantananda Puri

April 15, 2002
Vasishtha Guha – Himalayas

Introduction

Garland of Advaitic Wisdom is comprised of an introduction to Advaita Vedanta, followed by a large collection of crest non-dual teachings extracted from ancient scriptures of Advaita Vedanta, Zen Buddhism, Taoism, and also from the recorded teachings of Sri Ramana Maharshi.

The first part of the book accounts for the origin of Advaita, beginning with the *Veda*-s, the Indian philosophical systems, and concluding with Vedanta. A brief description of the Vedanta philosophical system follows, and then a detailed accounting of the fundamental doctrines of the Advaita School and its sub-schools, *Vivarana*, *Bhamati*, and *Varttika*. The first part of the book provides the reader with the minimal theoretical knowledge he needs for a correct understanding of the wisdom contained in the four parts of quotes.

In the second part of the book, the principal and largest section, the reader will find the essence of Advaita wisdom. Further, in part three, the reader will discover the wisdom of Sri Ramana Maharshi. In the last and shorter parts, four and five, the reader will find the wisdom of Zen and Tao.

The quotes selected and presented in these four parts are in the form of verses, sayings, and short stories. They were selected during the past five years and were chosen as best exemplifying the essential themes of the non-dualistic Eastern philosophies. To best enjoy and realize the wisdom of the quotes, the reader should keep in mind the principal themes covered in this book:

ॐ

❋ *Ajati-vada* ~ the doctrine of no-creation,

❋ *Paramartika-satya* ~ the Absolute Truth,

❋ *Brahman-jiva-jagat* ~ the identity of *Brahman,* the Absolute; *jiva*, the individual soul; and *jagat*, the phenomenal world,

❋ No-Time, No-Path ~ the realization of *Brahman* is ultimately beyond any factor of time, path or practice.

It is hoped that the reader will also enjoy the humorous quotes in Parts Two, Three, Four, and Five.

Following the five parts of the main body of the book are the Appendixes, which contain interesting and useful tables comparing the doctrines of Advaita and Vishishtadvaita Vedanta and also the tenets of the two principal schools of Advaita, *Vivarana*, and *Bhamati*. The Appendixes also contain variety of descriptive charts. Following the Appendixes there is a Glossary of important Sanskrit terms.

Though the quotes contained in this work represent the essence of the most important non-dual teachings, the serious spiritual seeker should make an effort to read and study the complete texts from which the quotes were taken.

May your study be well illumined and your understanding right and final! May you never discard *Brahman* and may *Brahman* never discard you!

OM Shanti!

Ajati

May 25, 2002
Tiruvannamalai - India

Transliteration of Sanskrit Terms

Sanskrit terms are rendered according to a simplified system of transliteration commonly used in non-scholarly works. The following differences will be noted between the scholarly form and the simple form used in this book:

Simple Form	Scholarly Form
ch (chakra)	c (cakra)
n (Sanskrit)	ṃ (Saṃskrit)
m (ahamkara)	ṃ (ahaṃkara)
Ri (Rig Veda)	Ṛ (Ṛg Veda)
Sh (Shiva; Krishna)	Ś, ṣ (Śiva; Kṛṣna)
t, d, n, h	ṭ, ḍ, ṇ, ḥ

The pronunciation of "v" is with the teeth lightly against the lower lip, so that the sound created is between the English "v" and "w".

ॐ

PART ONE

Advaita Vedanta
Origin and Doctrine

Vedas and Darshanas

Advaita Vedanta traces its origin and basic tenets back to the *Veda*-s, the most ancient and sacred scriptures of Hinduism. For Hindus, the *Veda*-s are the texts of uncontested authority; they are called *Shruti*-s (the heard texts) and regarded as *apaurusheya* (revealed but unauthored). The key message of the *Veda*-s is that one's real self – the very Self – is absolute, immortal, ever free, and pure. All other works in which the doctrines and practices of Hindus are encoded, are considered to have human authors and are known as *Smriti*-s (the remembered texts) and *Purana*-s (the ancient narratives).

There are four *Veda*-s and the first three are considered by Hindu tradition as principal and most important:

(1) *Rig Veda* ~ wisdom of the verses

(2) *Yajur Veda* ~ wisdom of the sacrificial formulas

(3) *Sama Veda* ~ wisdom of the musical chants

(4) *Atharva Veda* ~ wisdom of the *Atharvan* priests

Each of the four *Veda*-s contains four sections that came into existence at different periods of time. The first sections were the *Samhita*-s (collections), followed by the *Brahmana*-s (discussions of the rituals), then the *Aranyaka*-s (texts studied in the forest), and finally the *Upanishad*-s (secret teachings concerning *Brahman*, the Absolute). The elaboration in prose and verse of the Vedic literature stretches in time from the *Rig Veda* (c. 1400 BC.) to the *Upanishad*-s (c. 1000-500 BC.).

Ancient India gave birth to a great number of *rishi*-s (seers) and *acharya*-s (teachers) who founded and espoused a great variety of philosophical systems. This ancient tradition accounts for nine *darshana*-s (philosophical systems) which are classified into two groups:

I. The orthodox or *astika* group – those systems accepting the authority of the *Veda*-s:

(1) *Sankhya* (enumeration) ~ founded by Kapila

(2) *Yoga* (union) ~ founded by Patanjali

(3) *Nyaya* (logic) ~ founded by Gotama

(4) *Vaisheshika* (particular) ~ founded by Kanada

(5) *Mimamsa* (reflection) ~ founded by Jaimini

(6) *Vedanta* (conclusion of *Veda*) ~ founded by Badarayana

II. The heterodox or *nastika* group – those systems born as protest movements against the Vedic tradition:

(7) *Buddha-Dharma* ~ founded by Buddha

(8) *Jaina* ~ founded by Mahavira

(9) *Charvaka* ~ founded by Charvaka

Of these nine philosophical systems, *Vedanta Darshana* is the subject of the following chapter.

Vedanta

Vedanta is one of the six orthodox philosophical systems (*darshana*-s), and it forms the basis of many later movements of Indian philosophy and spiritual practice. In Sanskrit, Vedanta means the conclusion of the *Veda*-s. Other names for Vedanta are: *Vedanta Mimamsa* (reflection on *Vedanta*), *Uttara Mimamsa* (reflection on the latter part of the *Veda*-s), and *Brahma Mimamsa* (reflection on *Brahman*).

Triple Canon

The triple canon of Vedanta – the *Upanishad*-s, the *Brahma Sutra*, and the *Bhagavad Gita* – is called *Prasthanatraya*. The *Upanishad*-s constitute *Shruti-prasthana* (heard texts) and they mark the summit of the *Veda*-s, known as *Shruti*-s (heard texts). They are the pristine springs of Vedantic metaphysics and regarded as the most esteemed texts. The *Brahma Sutra* is *nyaya-prasthana* (text of logic) because it sets forth the teachings of Vedanta through use of logic. The third of the canonical texts, the *Bhagavad Gita*,

ॐ

has a status almost equal to that of the *Upanishad*-s. The *Bhagavad Gita* embodies the teachings of Sri Krishna, and is the philosophical summa, as well as the dramatic high point of the *Mahabharata*. Though part of the *Mahabharata,* which is an *Itihasa* (epic), the *Bhagavad Gita* is a *Smriti* (remembered text) and therefore called *Smriti-prasthana*.

The *Upanishad*-s are the conclusion of the *Veda*-s and they form the philosophical section of the *Veda*-s. As contrasted with the previous portions of the *Veda*-s (the *Samhita*-s, *Brahmana*-s, and *Aranyaka*-s), dealing with rituals and known as *karma-kanda*, the *Upanishad*-s are known as *jnana-kanda* because they deal with knowledge of the Absolute. The *Upanishad*-s also deserve their other name, *Brahma-kanda*, because they deal with *Brahman*.

The cardinal teachings of the *Upanishad*-s are the following:

(1) *Brahma-vidya* ~ wisdom concerning *Brahman*

(2) *Adhyatma-vidya* ~ wisdom of intuiting the all-pervading, all-comprehensive, all-extensive reality

(3) *Atmaikatva-vidya* ~ wisdom of intuiting the Oneness of *Atman*

(4) *Brahmatmaikatva-vidya* ~ wisdom of intuiting the identity of *Atman* with *Brahman*

(5) *Bhuma-vidya* ~ wisdom of intuiting the Infinite Reality

Each *Upanishad* is related to the *Veda* in which it appears and the Upanishadic teaching is often presented in the context of a particular Vedic hymn or ritual. There are thousands of *Upanishad*-s, but 108 are well-known and considered the most important by tradition. Recently this number has been expanded to 180 and published as the largest collection of

Upanishad-s. Scholars classify the *Upanishad*-s according to the subject matter they cover. Thus, there is a large number of Vedanta *Upanishad*-s dealing with the main topics of Vedanta and other *Upanishad*-s that concentrate on other subject-matters. The latter are the *Yoga Upanishad*-s, *Sannyasa Upanishad*-s, *Shaiva Upanishad*-s, *Vaishnava Upanishad*-s, and *Shakta Upanishad*-s.

Shankara and other teachers wrote commentaries on ten *Upanishad*-s, which have come to be considered the most important, and these are:

(1) *Aitareya Upanishad* ~ (*Rig Veda*)

(2) *Brihadaranyaka Upanishad* ~ (*Shukla Yajur Veda*)

(3) *Isavashya Upanishad* ~ (*Shukla Yajur Veda*)

(4) *Taittiriya Upanishad* ~ (*Krishna Yajur Veda*)

(5) *Katha Upanishad* ~ (*Krishna Yajur Veda*)

(6) *Chandogya Upanishad* ~ (*Sama Veda*)

(7) *Kena Upanishad* ~ (*Sama Veda*)

(8) *Mundaka Upanishad* ~ (*Atharva Veda*)

(9) *Mandukya Upanishad* ~ (*Atharva Veda*)

(10) *Prashna Upanishad* ~ (*Atharva Veda*)

Also to these ten, the *Kaushitaki Upanishad* (*Rig Veda*) and the *Svetashvatara Upanishad* (*Krishna Yajur Veda*) are usually added.

The *Brahma Sutra* is a great treatise of Vedanta, containing a collection of *sutra*-s or aphorisms (555 aphorisms, according to Shankara). Its appearance was a consequence of the fact that the *Upanishad*-s did not offer an entirely lucid picture of the various topics discussed by them. Since the Vedic tradition considers the *Upanishad*-s as one canonical scripture – the

Shruti – it became essential to reinterpret and reorganize their teachings, so as to give them more coherence and consistency of content; and the *Brahma Sutra* of Rishi Badarayana perfectly accomplished that goal.

The *Brahma Sutra* derives its name from the fact that it deals primarily with *Brahman*, the Absolute, as described in the *Upanishad*-s. This work is also known by other names: *Vedanta Sutra*, as it is the aphoristic text on Vedanta; *Shariraka Sutra*, because it is concerned with the nature and destiny of the embodied soul; *Bhikshu Sutra*, because those most competent to study it are the *bhikshu*-s *or sannyasin*-s (renunciates); and *Uttara Mimamsa Sutra*, as it is an enquiry into the latter sections of the *Veda*-s.

Very little is known about the author of this important work, Rishi Badarayana. Traditionally, he is identified as Rishi Vyasa, the author of the *Mahabharata* and the *Purana*-s, and therefore most scholars date the *Brahma Sutra* to the period 500 – 200 BC. However, some scholars consider that the two "Badarayana" were not one and the same person and date *Brahma Sutra* to a later period (c. 200 AD).

The *Bhagavad Gita* ("Song of the Lord") is one of the greatest and most beautiful of the Hindu scriptures. It is in the form of a dialogue between the warrior Prince Arjuna and his friend and charioteer *Krishna*, who is an *avatara* (incarnation) of *Vishnu*. The *Bhagavad Gita* forms part of Book VI of the *Mahabharata* ("The Great Epic of the Bharata Dynasty") and was probably written in the 1st or 2nd century AD. It is a poem consisting of 700 Sanskrit verses divided into 18 chapters. Chapters 1 to 6 deal with *karma-marga* (path of action), 7 to 12 with *bhakti-marga* (path of devotion), and the last six chapters, 13 to 18, teach *jnana-marga* (path of knowledge).

The popularity of the *Bhagavad Gita* is evident from the many commentaries, glossaries, and expository books written on it in both ancient and modern times. The earliest known commentary is that of Shankara. Other important commentaries of ancient times are those of Bhaskara, Ramanuja, Madhva, Nilakantha, Shridhara, Madhusudana, and Shankarananda.

Schools of Vedanta

Several schools of Vedanta have emerged as a result of different interpretations of the *Prasthana-traya* (the *Upanishad*-s, the *Brahma Sutra* and the *Bhagavad Gita*). These schools are differentiated principally by their views regarding the relationship and identity of the individual self (*jiva*) with the absolute (*Brahman*).

The classification of the different Vedantic schools is given below:

I. Non-dualistic Vedanta (Advaita) of Shankara and its three schools:

(1) *Vivarana* ~ founded by Padmapada

(2) *Bhamati* ~ founded by Vacaspati

(3) *Varttika* ~ founded by Sureshvara

II. Monotheistic Vedanta and its five *Vaishnava* schools:

(1) *Vishishtadvaita* ~ founded by Ramanuja

(2) *Dvaita* ~ founded by Madhva

(3) *Dvaitadvaita* ~ founded by Nimbarka

(4) *Shuddhadvaita* ~ founded by Vallabha

(5) *Achintya-Bhedabheda* ~ founded by Chaitanya

Among the above schools, Advaita (non-dualism) of the 8th century philosopher Shankara and two of the five schools of monotheism, Vishishtadvaita (qualified non-dualism) of the 11th century philosopher Ramanuja, and Dvaita (dualism) of the 13th century philosopher Madhva, are well known. These three constitute the main streams of Vedanta.

Though there are major philosophical differences between the schools of Vedanta, they do share a number of common concepts. One important point is that they unanimously reject the conclusions of the heterodox philosophical systems of *Buddha-Dharma*, *Jaina*, and *Charvaka*. They also reject the conclusions of the orthodox schools, *Nyaya*, *Vaisheshika*, *Sankhya*, *Yoga*, and to a lesser extent those of *Mimamsa*.

The influence of Vedanta on Indian thought has been so profound, that it may be said, that in one or another of its forms Indian philosophy has become essentially Vedanta.

Advaita (non-dualism) is the most influential of the schools of Vedanta. The main tenets of Advaita were first expressed in the *Upanishad*-s and later more clearly systematized in the *Brahma Sutra*. However, the formal beginning of Advaita is considered to be the great text *Mandukya Karika* of Gaudapada (c. 7-8th century), an explanatory text on the *Mandukya Upanishad*. Shankara (c. 788-820 AD.) greatly expanded the philosophy of Advaita, building on the foundation of Gaudapada's doctrine.

The body of Advaitic literature contains a very large number of works, and it may be noted that while *Mandukya Karika* is Gaudapada's sole known work, Shankara is credited with almost 300 works. The most important of these are considered Shankara's commentaries (*bhashya*-s) on the *Upanishad*-s, *Brahma Sutra*, and *Bhagavad Gita*, and his own original works, like *Vivekachudamani*, *Upadesha Sahasri*, *Aparokshanubhuti*, *Atmabodha*, etc. Other important Advaitic texts are *Yoga Vasishtha*, *Ashtavakra Gita*, and *Ribhu Gita*.

In modern times, due to the predominance of the Advaitic texts, it has become popular (especially in the West) to consider that Vedanta means strictly Advaita, but this is not correct. Advaita is not synonymous with Vedanta, but only one of the three main schools of it. However, from the time of Rishi Badarayana and through the time of Gaudapada and Shankara, up until the appearance of the Vishishtadvaita School, Vedanta could correctly be identified as solely Advaita. But this equation does not apply today.

Vishishtadvaita (qualified non-dualism) is the second important school of Vedanta. It grew out of the *Vaishnava* (sect of god *Vishnu*) devotional movement prominent in South India from the 7th century on. The most towering figure of this movement was Ramanuja (c. 1055-1137 AD.), who wrote a commentary on the *Brahma Sutra*, the *Shri Bhashya* ("Beautiful Commentary"), and on the *Bhagavad Gita,* as well as a treatise on the *Upanishad*-s, the *Vedarthasamgraha* ("Summary of the Meaning of the *Veda*").

Ramanuja admits that there is non-duality and an ultimate identity of the trinity – God, the individual soul, and the phenomenal world – but this non-duality is postulated of God, who is qualified (*vishishta*) by matter and soul; hence his doctrine is known as Vishishtadvaita (qualified non-dualism) as opposed to the non-dualism of Shankara.

Ramanuja was the first philosopher of Vedanta to equate *Narayana* (a personal God) with *Brahman* (the Absolute) of the *Upanishad*-s. As a personal God, *Narayana* possesses all auspicious qualities to a perfect degree, and Ramanuja does not tire of mentioning these qualities. He interprets the relationship between the non-dual and infinite *Narayana* and the plural and finite creation in an original way, and his interpretation has some support in the *Upanishad*-s. For him, the relation between the infinite and the finite is analogous to that between the soul and the body; non-duality is primary but differences can still exist; soul and matter are totally dependent on God for their existence, as is the body on the soul.

ॐ

In Vishishtadvaita, God has two aspects: cause (Creator) and effect (the phenomenal world). As cause He is essence qualified only by His divine perfections; as effect He is His body constituted of *jiva*-s (individual souls) and *jagat* (phenomenal world). For Ramanuja, release from bondage is not the dry and radical end of *samsara* (cycle of birth, death, and rebirth) but rather the joy of the contemplation of God. This joy is attained by a life of exclusive *bhakti* (devotion) to God: singing His praise, performing devotional acts in temples, private worship, and constantly dwelling on His perfections. In return God will bestow His grace, which will assist the devotee in attaining *moksha* (liberation).

According to the Vishishtadvaita School liberation can be of five types:

(1) *Sarupya* ~ the liberated has an identical form with God

(2) *Salokya* ~ the liberated lives in the same world with God

(3) *Samipya* ~ the liberated lives as a very close attendant of God

(4) *Sarshti* ~ the liberated possesses all *siddhi*-s (supernatural powers) of God excepting the power to create

(5) *Sayujya* ~ the liberated becomes one with God

Vishishtadvaita flourished after Ramanuja, but a schism developed over the importance of God's grace. For the southern, Sanskrit-using school, the *Vadakalai*, God's grace in attaining liberation is important but man must also put forth his best efforts. This school is represented by the thinker Venkatanatha, who was known by the honorific name of *Vedantadeshika* (Teacher of Vedanta). For the northern, Tamil-using school, the *Tenkalai*, God's grace alone is necessary and sufficient for the attainment of liberation.

The influence of Vishishtadvaita spread far to the north, where it played a role in the devotional renaissance of Vaishnavism.

ॐ

The doctrines promoted by Ramanuja still inspire a lively intellectual tradition, and the religious practices he emphasized are still carried on in the two most important *Vaishnava* centers in southern India: *Ranganatha* temple in Shrirangam, Tamil Nadu State, and *Venkateshvara* temple in Tirupati, Andhra Pradesh State.

Dvaita (dualism) is the third important school of Vedanta. Its founder Madhva, also called Anandatirtha (c. 1199-1278), came from the area of modern Karnataka State, where even today he continues to have many followers. During his lifetime Madhva was regarded by his followers as an incarnation of the god *Vayu*, who had been sent to earth by Lord *Vishnu* to save the world, after the powers of evil had sent the philosopher Shankara, the promoter of the Advaita School.

Madhva shows in his expositions the influence of the *Nyaya* philosophy. He asserts that *Vishnu* is the supreme God, thus identifying *Brahman* of the *Upanishad*-s with a personal God, as Ramanuja had done before him. In Madhva's system there are three eternal, ontological orders: God, soul, and insentient nature. The existence of God is provable by logic, though only scripture teaches His nature. He is the quintessence of all perfections and possesses a non-material body which consists of *Sat-Cit-Ananda* (absolute existence, consciousness, and bliss). Madhva affirms that God is the efficient cause of the universe but denies that he is the material cause. God cannot be the material cause of the world, either by splitting or transforming Himself, because this goes against the principle of a changeless and indivisible God, and it is blasphemous to accept that a perfect God changes Himself into an imperfect phenomenal world.

Jiva-s (individual souls) are countless in number and are of atomic size; they are "parts" of God and exist completely by His grace and their actions are entirely subject to His will. Yet, God also allows the soul, to a limited extent, freedom of action; freedom qualified by and in proportion to the soul's past *karma*-s (actions).

For Madhva, as for many other Indian philosophers, *ajnana* (ignorance) is erroneous knowledge. It can be removed by means of *bhakti* (devotion). Devotion is attained in various ways: by solitary study of the scriptures, by performing one's duty with complete detachment, or by devotional acts. Devotion brings intuitive insight into, or a special kind of knowledge of, God's nature. *Bhakti* may itself become the goal; for the devotee, adoration of *Vishnu* is more important than the liberation that results from it.

The present-day school of Dvaita has as its center a complex, consisting of a temple dedicated to Lord *Krishna* and six *matha*-s (monasteries), located in Udipi, Karnataka State. This center was founded by Madhva himself and continues under an uninterrupted line of successors.

Advaita

Advaita is one of the schools of Vedanta and well known as a non-dualistic philosophy. It is a philosophy because it makes an enquiry into Truth and Reality but, in contrast to the other *darshana*-s (philosophical systems), it reveals the Truth that is not subject to modification in space and time, but rather is the ultimate, non-dual, and changeless Reality, certainly verified and verifiable.

Advaita is also known as the Science of Reality (*Brahma-vidya*), and in its investigation it makes use of six means of attaining valid knowledge – perception, inference, verbal testimony, analogy, indirect inference, and non-apprehension – and covers all states and conditions through which life passes.

Advaita Lineage

In the Advaita School of Vedanta the *Guru-Parampara* (lineage of *guru*-s) broadly lists: Narayana, Padmabhuva (*Brahma*), Vasishtha, Shakti, Parasara, Vyasa, Shuka, Dakshinamurti, Gaudapada, Govinda, Shankara, Sureshvara Padmapada, Hastamalaka, Totaka, and others.

The Indian philosophical and religious tradition traces *Brahma-vidya* (knowledge of *Brahman*) back to the gods and to the *rishi*-s who had the revelation of the *Veda*-s. Thus, the Advaita *Guru-Parampara* begins with the *Daiva-Parampara*, represented by Narayana and Padmabhuva (*Brahma*); followed by the *Rishi-Parampara*, which includes the Vedic seers Vasishtha, Shakti, Parasara, his son Vyasa, Shuka (son of Vyasa), and Dakshinamurti; and the *Manava-Parampara* (the contemporaries of Manu, the law-maker), which lists the preceptors Gaudapada, Govinda, Shankara, Sureshvara, Padmapada, Totaka, and Hastamalaka; and others. These human *guru*-s are regarded as incarnations of various deities, and their traditional accounts are recorded in the *Shankaradigvijaya* texts.

But, in a strict sense, the tradition of *guru*-s in Advaita commences with Dakshinamurti, continues with Shankara, and is followed by his four famous disciples, Sureshvara, Padmapada, Totaka, and Hastamalaka. The Advaita *Guru-Parampara* has continued to this day through the succession of *Shankaracharya*-s, as well as other *guru*-s and *sannyasin*-s of Shankara's order.

Traditionally, Gaudapada, Shankara and two of his disciples, Padmapada and Sureshvara, are regarded as the most important figures in Advaita.

Doctrines of Advaita

Essential to Shankara's Advaita is the tenet that *Brahman* is the Reality and the world is unreal. Any change, duality, or plurality – whether subjective or objective – is only a superimposition (*adhyasa*) on *Brahman*, which comes about through *avidya* (ignorance) and *maya* (illusive power).

Brahman is outside time, space, and causality, which are simply forms of empirical experience, and such experiences are illusory and completely unreal. Shankara, in all his works, firmly proclaims that *moksha* is the realization of the identity of *jiva*, *Atman*, and *Brahman*; and that *Brahman* is, in truth, all that exists; and that no distinction in *Brahman* or from *Brahman* is ever possible.

These tenets are the heart of Shankara's teaching and are dealt with in the following pages.

Brahman

According to Advaita there is only one Absolute Reality. It is called *Brahman*. A classical sentence defining *Brahman* appears in *Taittiriya Upanishad*, II. 1. 3: "*satyam jnanam anantam brahma* ", which means "*Brahman is Reality-Knowledge-Infinity*". Shankara identifies *Brahman* with pure consciousness or the witness, whose non-existence cannot be conceived or imagined, and which is not subject to any change, for the witness of change remains unchanged. The knowledge of *Brahman*, the Absolute Reality, is the truest and the highest that an earnest seeker can or need attain.

Advaita is distinguished from other schools of thought (monotheistic or dualistic) by its assertion that *Brahman* is the non-dual Reality, without attributes, and one with *Atman* and *jiva* (the individual self). This central Advaitic doctrine is best expressed by Shankara's famous statement: "*brahma satyam jagat mithya jivo brahmaiva na parah*", meaning "*Brahman* is real, the universe is illusory, and *jiva* is non-different from *Brahman*".

A question arises in the mind of every seeker of truth: What is reality? Advaita gives the following clear answer: Reality is That which remains absolutely unchanged through all time (past, present, and future) and in all space, as well as during the three states (waking, dreaming, and sleeping).

Advaita further states that *Brahman*, the Reality, is one without a second; hence, it is called *advaya* (non-dual). This term should not however be considered as the absence of duality, or as something other than duality, or as something opposed to duality. Rather, *advaya* means the All, the Whole; where "All" is free of quantity or number and "Whole" is not composed of parts or of separate things bundled together.

Maya and Avidya

How does *Brahman*, the Absolute and indivisible Reality, appear divided into innumerable beings and countless objects?

The *Upanishad*-s explain that *maya* (illusive power) causes the appearance of *jagat* (the universe) and *avidya* (ignorance) causes *Brahman* to appear as a multitude of *jiva*-s (individual souls). *Maya* operates at the cosmic level while *avidya* operates at the individual level. In a primal sense *maya* is the illusive power (the cause) that creates the universe, and in a secondary sense it is the universe itself (the effect).

An important and interesting aspect of *avidya* (ignorance) is its two-fold power or *shakti*, namely *avarana-shakti* (veiling power) and *vikshepa-shakti* (projecting power). *Avarana-shakti* veils *Atman*'s true nature and *vikshepa-shakti* accounts for the appearance of *jiva* by apparently transforming *Atman*. Such an apparent effect is a *vivarta* (an apparent transformation) of the original object and the theory of apparent transformation is known as *vivarta-vada*.

Shankara describes *avidya* as *anadi* (beginningless) and *anirvachaniya* (indefinable) and warns that seeking the roots of *avidya* is itself nothing but an expression of the very *avidya* which the seeker wants to remove.

ॐ

Regarding *avidya,* Shankara makes a very clear and final affirmation: *avidya* is responsible for *kama* (desires) and *karma* (action), which leads to *bandha* (bondage). Thus, he states that complete cancellation of *avidya* will lead to *moksha* (liberation) or the non-dual state of *Brahman.*

Jiva

The limited *Atman* or the embodied self is called *jiva,* the individual soul. Due to inexplicable ignorance (*avidya*) the *Atman* or *Brahman,* whose nature is *Sat-Cit-Ananda* (Absolute Existence-Consciousness-Bliss), finds itself caught up in the body-mind complex. This *Atman* in bondage, the *jiva* (individual soul), being in possession of five *kosha*-s (sheaths) and three *sharira*-s (bodies), lives and acts in the world driven by numerous desires. Experiencing pleasure and pain due to past *karma*-s (actions), *jiva* is subject to *samsara* (cycle of birth, death, and rebirth) until the attainment of *moksha* (liberation).

Shankara makes clear that when *jiva* is devoid of its *upadhi*-s (limiting adjuncts) – like ignorance, the mind, and the body – it is completely identical with *Brahman,* having *Sat-Cit-Ananda* (Absolute Existence-Consciousness-Bliss) as its sole nature.

Adhyasa and Anirvachaniya

If *Brahman* is the sole reality, one without a second, and identical with *Atman* and *jiva,* then how and why does the *jiva* fail to recognize its own non-dual reality but instead perceives the phenomenal world of names and forms (*namarupa*-s)?

Advaita explains this dilemma through *anirvachaniya-khyati,* the theory of indefinable erroneous cognition. The classical example is given by Shankara: the seeing of a snake in a rope in poor light. In this example there is a false perception of the snake, which in fact is only the impression of a snake from an earlier idea of the same, superimposed upon the rope under conditions favorable to the error. Thus, *adhyaropa* or *adhyasa* (superimposition) is responsible for *mithya-jnana* (erroneous or false knowledge). And so is *Brahman* mistakenly perceived as the world of names and forms.

The snake (or the world) is neither real (*sat*) nor unreal (*asat*). It is not completely unreal like "the son of a barren woman" since it is perceived; nor is it real since it vanishes as soon as the rope (or *Brahman*), the substratum, is perceived or known as it is. Therefore, with the purpose of giving a logical explanation to such an atypical phenomenon, Shankara creates a third category of perceived objects, namely *sad-asad-vilakshana* (different from both the real and the unreal). *Khyati* or the cognition of such an object is described as *anirvachaniya* or indefinable.

Vivarta and Parinama

Two major theories are used to explain the material cause of the world:

(1) *Vivarta-vada* ~ the theory of apparent transformation

(2) *Parinama-vada* ~ the theory of real transformation

Causality in which the material cause itself does not change into something else is called *vivarta*. For example, gold is the material cause of ornaments made of gold. Following the process of creating ornaments the gold does not lose its nature and does not get transformed into a different metal. The original gold is only reshaped into another form, from a mass into an ornament; but gold remains gold. In Advaita this theory is promoted by Shankara and his followers. Causality in which

🕉

the material cause involves real change is called *parinama*. For example, milk is the material cause of curd; in the process of curdling the milk becomes curd and the original state of the milk is irrecoverably lost. This theory is promoted by the *Sankhya* philosophy and is often analyzed and refuted in classical texts of Advaita.

From the highest point of view both theories of causality, *parinama-vada* and *vivarta-vada*, are unsatisfactory, as they are applicable only when the concept of creation is accepted as a real fact. The final and most subtle conclusion of Advaita is *ajati-vada* (the theory of no-creation) which states that there is no causality or creation at all, but only the unchanging Reality. In the *Upanishad*-s this conclusion is clearly supported by numerous passages that affirm that *Brahman* is ever changeless and partless.

Three Degrees of Reality

Shankara does not really accept multiple realities or truths. Nevertheless, for the sake of seekers, to offer a gradual understanding of his ultimate position, he speaks of three degrees of reality:

(1) *Paramarthika-satya* ~ the Absolute Reality

(2) *Pratibhasika-satya* ~ the illusory reality

(3) *Vyavaharika-satya* ~ the empirical reality

Paramarthika-satya is the non-dual *Brahman,* the Absolute and ever existent. *Pratibhasika-satya* is the erroneous appearance of something where it does not exist (like the snake in the rope), which disappears as soon as the obstacles to the correct knowledge are removed. *Vyavaharika-satya* is the empirical universe of names, forms, and experiences, which lasts until *Brahman* is realized.

These three levels of reality correspond to different grades of spiritual seekers. For the most advanced seekers *Paramarthika-satya* always stands as the only accepted reality.

Three Theories of Creation

In the tradition of Advaita the creation of the universe is explained by three fundamental theories:

(1) *Ajati-vada* ~ the doctrine of no-creation

(2) *Drishti-srishti-vada* ~ the doctrine of simultaneous perception and creation

(3) *Srishti-drishti-vada* ~ the doctrine of gradual creation and perception

Ajati doctrine is an expression of *paramarthika-satya* (the Absolute Reality), *drishti-srishti* doctrine is an expression of *pratibhasika-satya* (the illusory reality), and *srishti-drishti* doctrine an expression of *vyavaharika-satya* (the empirical reality).

The *shishya* (disciple) begins the path with firm belief in *srishti-drishti-vada*, then continues with *drishti-srishti-vada*, and finally reaches the summit with the comprehension of *ajati-vada*. At this point he understands that no creation ever happened and that *Brahman* is the only changeless reality.

The *guru*, in instructing a disciple, may insist on one or another of these doctrines depending upon his own views, the capacity of the disciple, and other factors.

Ajati-vada (also called *ajata-vada*) first appeared in *Ashtavakra Gita*, and later was elaborated and fully revealed by Gaudapada, Shankara's *paramaguru* (grandteacher), in his exquisite work *Mandukya Karika*. Verse 32 of the second part (*Vaitathya Prakarana*) of *Mandukya Karika* is universally accepted as the most representative of this doctrine: "*There is no dissolution, no birth, none in bondage and none aspiring for wisdom, no seeker of liberation and none liberated. This is the Absolute Truth*". Of all the three theories of creation this is regarded as the absolute and final view and is suitable only for the most advanced students.

According to *ajati-vada*, *Brahman* is the birthless and changeless Reality. Therefore, the three fundamental principles considered in other doctrines, namely *jagat*, *jiva*, and *Ishvara*, are completely denied, leaving no room for discussion.

The second view, *drishti-srishti-vada*, was advocated by Prakasananda Sarasvati (c. 15-16th century) in his work *Vedanta-Siddhanta-Muktavali*. Gaudapada also used a similar view in *Mandukya Karika*, in his exposition leading to *ajati-vada*. This view is close to that of many schools of subjective idealism and to the view of the idealistic school of Mahayana Buddhism, Yogachara.

In essence, the view of *drishti-srishti-vada* is that *Jagat* (world), *jiva* (individual soul), and *Ishvara* (personal God) are all cognized and created simultaneously by the seer only and they do not have any existence apart from the seer. This view is connected to what is known as *eka-jiva-vada* (the doctrine of the existence of only one soul) and cannot be viewed independently of it. Ultimately there is only one seer or one self, who is identical with *Brahman*, who creates and sees the world simultaneously. Therefore, anything other than the seer is nothing but a myth.

Srishti-drishti-vada is the view of gradual creation and knowledge of it. It admits, more or less, the existence of the Absolute Reality underlying the entire Creation, which is the play of *maya*, the creative power of God (*Ishvara*). Perceiving the world of names and forms in all its variety, the *jiva* believes itself to be the subject and also presumes a Creator for everything. Thus, all is reduced to three fundamental principles: *jagat* (the world), *jiva* (the individual soul), and

Ishvara (the personal God). A *jiva* discovers the existence of God and makes use of right means to know Him in order to attain salvation; however, after a *jiva* is liberated there always remain other *jiva*-s (individuals in bondage) who should follow the path and attain their own release. This view is found not only in Advaita but in all major religions and philosophical systems describing gradual creation, spiritual evolution, and liberation.

In Advaita the two temporary views of creation, *drishti-srishti-vada* and *srishti-drishti-vada*, are offered to those students who have a strong belief in creation.

Pramanas and Jnana

In Indian philosophy *pramana*-s are defined as means of attaining valid knowledge (*prama*). Each *pramana* has a distinctive way of transmitting and presenting a different type of knowledge, without contradicting any other *pramana*. Advaita recognizes six *pramana*-s:

(1) *Pratyaksha* ~ perception

(2) *Anumana* ~ inference

(3) *Agama* or *sabda* ~ verbal testimony

(4) *Upamana* ~ analogy

(5) *Arthapatti* ~ indirect inference

(6) *Anupalabdhi* ~ non-apprehension

The most important means of knowledge is *pratyaksha* (perception) and it is of two kinds: external and internal. Perception by any of the five senses (hearing, sight, touch, smell, and taste) is considered external, while any kind of mental perception (of knowledge and ignorance, pleasure and pain, love and hate, etc.) is considered internal.

External perception coming through the senses is the normal and direct way of knowing the external world.

Internal perception is of two types: (1) concerning the perceiving self and (2) concerning the states of the mind.

An example of the latter is a person experiencing ignorance, which is a mental state. He is aware of himself as the experiencer or the perceiving self, as is evident from such expressions as "I feel ignorant" and "I am ignorant". Nevertheless, he identifies himself with the mental state despite the fact that he is the perceiving self and separate from it (the mental state). Though the Self shines in Itself and is free of subject-object relation and every person is more or less aware of himself as the experiencer, yet, due to ignorance (*avidya*), everybody fails in clear self-recognition or permanent self-awareness. Likewise, though a knower of the body and the mind, a person becomes identified with the known and believes himself to be the body-mind complex, subject to birth, growth, decay, death, hunger and thirst, pain and pleasure, etc. The failure to hold awareness of the self amidst experience remains until right knowledge is attained.

Right knowledge regarding the witness-self and its identity with the Absolute Self is revealed by the *Shruti*-s (*Upanishad*-s) and other ancient texts. When the seeker applies such knowledge, he becomes progressively aware of his true nature and concludes with *aparokshanubhuti*, the intuitive realization of the Self as non-dual consciousness or *Brahman*.

In Advaita the intuitive knowledge or intuitive realization is properly regarded as the crest of all knowledge and not a means (*pramana*) to its attainment.

ॐ

Thus the most important means of knowledge, perception (*pratyaksha*), is concerned with a triad: (1) the Pure Self, (2) mental states, and (3) material objects.

Advaita further states that valid knowledge (*prama*) has two aspects: (1) Pure Consciousness (*shuddha-chaitanya*) and (2) modal consciousness (*vritti-chaitanya*). Knowledge as Pure Consciousness is considered metaphysical knowledge, whereas modal consciousness is considered empirical knowledge. The term knowledge (*jnana*) is generally used in the empirical sense of modal consciousness (*vritti-chaitanya* or *vritti-jnana*) and not in the sense of Pure Consciousness (*shuddha-chaitanya*).

Pure and self-shining Consciousness, being non-dual and always free of the subject-object relation, is the very essence or substance of the Self (*Atman*) and not an attribute. Pure Being and Pure Consciousness are one and the same. The self-existent cannot but be self-known; it is self-proofed. In truth, neither beingness nor consciousness can be studied separately.

The nature of modal consciousness or knowledge (*jnana*) is revelatory. It does not create, it discovers; it does not construct or transform anything, it apprehends all as it is. It has one and exclusive purpose – to unveil what is.

Anubhava, Tarka, and Shruti

In proclaiming and attaining the Absolute Truth an Advaitin makes use of the triple criteria: scripture (*Shruti*), reasoning (*tarka*), and intuitive realization (*anubhava*).

Of these three, intuitive realization (*anubhava*) of Reality delivers the highest degree of certitude, although it gives a lesser degree of conceptual clarity. In matters regarding supersensual reality, reasoning alone does not deliver certainty, for every argument established by reasoning is countered by an opposite argument supported by equally strong reasoning. The objective of scriptures is to teach and transmit the knowledge of *Brahman* through language and logic. But paradoxically, the *rishi*-s, realizers of the Absolute Reality, communicate through scripture what language and logic were not designed to communicate. In consequence, the seeker, making use of language and logic and having no direct experience of Reality, must take on faith the sacred texts and trust in their revelatory power for they record the highest experiences of those who struggled to realize the Absolute Reality.

Intuitive realization (*anubhava*) of the seers is the vital spiritual experience and is communicated only through scripture (*Shruti*), the written code embodying it.

Scriptural testimony is valid knowledge because it embodies the results of the realizers of Truth, which are always open to confirmation by the Self-Realization of new seekers of Truth. To accept *Shruti* is to recognize the highest wisdom of the saints and sages. To ignore *Shruti* is to turn a blind eye to the most elevated spiritual experience of mankind.

Spiritual realization is a great matter and is never the fruit of casual research and effort. In physical science one studies and apprehends what great researchers have verified; in music one studies and practices arduously what great composers have written. Likewise, in matters of Truth one listens to and considers deeply what great philosophers and religious seers have communicated of their understanding and experience.

The authority of scriptures is derived from the fact that they are the expression of Self-Realization. They are considered to be their own proof, requiring no support from elsewhere.

In conclusion, the *Shruti* as a source of knowledge is eternal. Its subject and final truth stands firm and complete and cannot be turned aside by speculation of any individual in the past, present, or future.

Reasoning (*tarka*), which works as an auxiliary of scripture (*Shruti*) and intuition (*anubhava*), is a critical tool against untested assumptions and also a creative principle which selects and emphasizes the facts of Truth. Shankara recognizes the need of reasoning for testing scriptural views, but also declares that reasoning should be allowed freedom so long as it does not conflict with the scriptures. The sacred scriptures, embodying the experience of universal truth, should be accepted as most authoritative. Any individualistic reasoning should be subordinated to the truth of scripture, since individualistic reasoning alone cannot lead to the establishment of truth on account of the endless diversity of limited individual apprehension.

Reasoning is a helpful guide to a certain extent. However, it is predominantly a 'negative' instrument and its findings are limited accordingly. It helps discard and negate what is false, but for realization of the Truth it is inadequate. Philosophy, which relies absolutely upon reasoning, has never been successful in positive findings. Its attempts in the latter area remain debatable and fail to command universal acceptance.

The Truth realized through scripture (*Shruti*), intuitive realization (*anubhava*), and reasoning (*tarka*), must always be identical, uncontradictable, and universal. All scriptural statements must conform to intuitive realization and be confirmed by deep and discerning reasoning.

Through application of the triple criteria discussed above, the seeker can successfully realize the falsity of duality, the falsity of everything that is presented as an other to consciousness.

Mahavakyas

The most classical, essential, and treasured teachings of Advaita are found in the *Upanishad*-s and are encapsulated as four great sentences or *mahavakya*-s. These are pure non-dual statements, identifying the individual soul (*jiva*) or limited consciousness with *Brahman*, the Absolute Consciousness.

(1) *Aham Brahmasmi* ~ "I am *Brahman*"

This *mahavakya* is found in *Yajur Veda, Brihadaranyaka Upanishad*, I.4.10. It states the absolute identity of *jiva*, the individual soul, with *Atman* and *Brahman*.

(2) *Ayam Atma Brahma* ~ "This *Atman* is *Brahman*"

This *mahavakya* is found in *Atharva Veda, Mandukya Upanishad*, 2. It also states the identity of *Atman* with *Brahman*, but in a less direct and more objective way.

(3) *Tat Tvam Asi* ~ "That you are"

This *mahavakya* is found in *Sama Veda, Chandogya Upanishad*, VI.8.7. It declares that the Absolute *Brahman* is identical with one's self, *jiva*, or *Atman*.

(4) *Prajnanam Brahma* ~ "Consciousness is *Brahman*"

This *mahavakya* is found in *Rig Veda, Aitareya Upanishad*, V.3. It identifies the consciousness present within the individual and the entire universe with *Brahman*, the Absolute.

In addition to the four *mahavakya*-s, another two sentences expressing the non-dual truth are well known and used as classical non-dual teaching.

(1) *Sarvam Khalvidam Brahma* ~ "All this is *Brahman*"

This sentence is found in *Sama Veda, Chandogya Upanishad* III.14.1. It teaches that the entire universe is nothing

ॐ

but the Absolute Reality, *Brahman*. The 'All' is charged with absolute meaning and includes God, the phenomenal world, individual soul, mind, body, ignorance and knowledge, time and space, and everything else known and unknown.

(2) *So' Ham* ~ "I am That"

This is the mantra repeated through the sound made by the natural movement of the breath. It shows the identity of the individual soul (*jiva*) with *Brahman*. "*So*" is the natural sound of inhalation and represents *Brahman*, while "*Ham*" is the sound of exhalation and represents *jiva*.

Sadhana

Shankara declares that the main obstacle to the *jiva*'s liberation (*moksha*) is the false identification (*tadatmya*) of the Self (*Atman*) with the body-mind complex resulting from superimposition (*adhyasa*). Therefore, the right way to remove the obstacle and attain *moksha* is to remove the false identification. This removal is accomplished by the reverse process of desuperimposition (*apavada*).

The traditional texts declare that the aspirant to *moksha* (liberation) must possess *sadhana-chatustaya* (four prerequisite disciplines for enlightenment):

(1) *Viveka* ~ discrimination

(2) *Vairagya* ~ renunciation

(3) *Samadi-shatka* ~ the group of six spiritual sub-disciplines: *shama* (tranquility of mind), *dama* (control of senses), *uparati* (cessation of senses), *titiksha* (forbearance of the pairs of opposites), *samadhana* (concentration of mind), and *shraddha* (faith in scriptural truth)

(4) *Mumukshutva* ~ desire for liberation

Discrimination (*viveka*) is a must for the student who follows *jnana-kanda* (section of knowledge). He should remember the most important kinds of *viveka*:

(1) *Avasthatraya viveka* ~ discrimination between the three states – waking, dreaming and deep sleep – and *Turiya*, the fourth. This *viveka* is said to be the most important. Reality is realized when the three states are known as unreal. Through negation of the three, the transcendental *Turiya* is arrived at.

(2) *Nityanitya vastu viveka* ~ discrimination of the real from the non-real.

(3) *Drik-drishya viveka* ~ discrimination of the seer from the seen.

(4) *Panchakosha viveka* ~ discrimination of the five sheaths from the *Atman*.

When the student possesses the four prerequisite disciplines for enlightenment (*sadhana-chatustaya*) he should approach a *guru* (teacher) who is established in *Brahman* and well versed in the sacred scriptures of Vedanta. Then he learns the truth from his *guru* by means of *shravana* (hearing), *manana* (reflection), and *nididhyasana* (deep meditation).

The most important part of learning the teaching is hearing, reflection, and deep meditation on the four *mahavakyas* (the great sentences).

Hearing (*shravana*) the *mahavakya*-s involves determining their correct meaning from scriptures by applying the *shadvidha-linga*-s (the six characteristic signs): *upakrama-upasamhara* (beginning and conclusion), *apurvata* (originality), *phala* (fruit or result), *arthavada* (eulogy), *abhyasa* (repetition), and *upapatti* (reasoning, demonstration).

By reflection (*manana*) the student achieves the deep conviction that he is not the body-mind complex but the *Atman* (the Self). In this stage he maintains steady identification with *Atman-Brahman* by removing the limiting adjuncts, like ignorance and the body-mind complex.

The veiling power of *ajnana* (*avarana-shakti*) has two distinct effects:

(1) *Asattvapadaka* ~ hiding the existence of *Brahman*

(2) *Abhanapadaka* ~ hiding the revelation of *Brahman*

The first effect of the veiling power is removed by the knowledge of *Brahman* resulting from *shravana* (hearing) and *manana* (reflection). The seeker becomes convinced of the existence of *Brahman* but still does not have the direct knowledge of *Brahman*. The second effect of the veiling power is removed by *brahmakara-vritti* (mental modification in the form of *Brahman*) generated by *nididhyasana* (deep meditation) on a *mahavakya*.

Throughout the stage of *nididhyasana*, when the seeker meditates on a *mahavakya* (for example "I am *Brahman*"), in his mind arises a mental modification (*vritti*) which makes him feel that he is *Brahman*. This special *vritti*, being opposed to all ordinary *vritti*-s, is called *brahmakara-vritti* (mental modification in the form of *Brahman*). *Brahmakara-vritti*, being illumined by the Absolute Consciousness of *Brahman*, destroys other mental modifications (like those of ignorance, doubt, etc.) and their effects (the different mental states). At this stage, *Brahman* is present only as *brahmakara-vritti* or special state of mind. But, following the removal of all other mental modifications and mental states, this mental state of *Brahman*, being left alone and overwhelmed by the Absolute Consciousness or *Brahman*, is absorbed and finally dissolved in It.

Thus, the mental state of *Brahman* vanishes and what remains is pure *Brahman* alone. This realization is *moksha* (liberation).

Moksha

Moksha, or liberation from *samsara* (cycle of birth, death, and rebirth), is not a perfection to be achieved but rather the reality of one's own self to be realized; and it is realized through the removal of the ignorance that conceals it.

Shankara gives the following two definitions of *moksha*, which in fact mean the same thing:

(1) *Brahma-bhava* ~ the realization of *Brahman*

(2) *Avidya-nivritti* ~ the cancellation of ignorance

For *Atman*, who is in truth ever free, the question of bondage and release does not arise at all. The ever-free Self only appears to be limited, to be a doer, and to be subject to *samsara* (cycle of birth, death, and rebirth); and these limitations constitute bondage. Immediate intuitive self-knowledge removes *avidya* (ignorance) and the Self is realized as infinite and ever-free; this is Liberation. The Self is neither bound nor liberated, only ignorance appears and disappears. The Self was, is, and will always be the ever-free Reality.

Although the change from ignorance to Self-knowledge requires steps on a temporal path, paradoxically time does not really play a role in the appearance of ignorance and its cancellation, since any limitation of the unlimited *Atman* is false at all times; knowledge of the Self and removal of ignorance are simultaneous. Thus, cancellation of ignorance, immediate Realization of *Brahman*, and Liberation are one and the same thing.

Direct intuitive knowledge of the Absolute Reality (*aparokshanubhuti*) does not produce an effect called liberation, but only removes the apparent veil of ignorance. Thus, Liberation is nothing but the cessation of ignorance.

Jivanmukti and Videhamukti

It must be noted that Liberation is only one, in the sense of freedom from bondage; but it can have two facets corresponding to the continuation or cessation of the physical body. *Moksha* attained while still in the body is known as *jivan-mukti* (liberation while alive). *Moksha* attained after the termination of *prarabdha-karma* (actions that create and sustain the body) and the falling off of the body is known as *videha-mukti* (liberation after death).

A very important point in Shankara's doctrine is that Liberation is possible while one has physical existence. Since bondage is not the existence or continuation of the body, but only the false identification of the Self with it, Shankara proclaims that the attainment of liberation is only the removal of the ignorance, or the false identification with the body, and not the falling off of the body.

Schools of Advaita

Though Shankara clearly enunciated the main doctrines of Advaita, some of them admitted more than one interpretation, and the result in the post-Shankara period was the emergence of a vast body of Advaitic literature leading to different *prasthana*-s (schools of thought). The best-known schools are the *Vivarana*, *Bhamati*, and *Varttika*.

Vivarana Prasthana is at present the most important school of Advaita and was promoted by one of the four disciples of Shankara, Padmapada (8th century A.D.), and later by Prakashatma (12th century A.D.). The name *vivarana* comes from the title *Pancapadikavivarana* of Prakashatma, which is a lengthy commentary on Padmapada's work *Panchapadika*.

The following commentaries and sub-commentaries are some of the important texts which define the Vivarana School:

- *Panchapadika* ~ Padmapada
- *Panchapadikavivarana* ~ Prakashatma
- *Tattvadipana* ~ Akhandananda
- *Tatparyadipika* ~ Chitsukha
- *Vivarana Tika* ~ Anandapurna Vidyasagara
- *Rjuvivarana* ~ Sarvajnavishnu

- *Darpana* ~ Rangaraja Dikshita
- *Darpana* ~ Amalananda
- *Padayojana* ~ Dharmaraja Adhvarindra

The principal tenets of the Vivarana School are:

- *Avidya* is *bhavarupa*, a positive something, but not real (*satya*) since it can be destroyed by knowledge.

- *Avidya* is the material (*upadana*) cause of the world, being a *jadatmika-shakti* (a force of material nature).

- *Avidya* is the efficient (*nimitta*) cause of the world in the capacity of being an error.

- *Avidya* possesses a twofold power: veiling (*avarana-shakti*) and projecting (*vikshepa-shakti*).

- *Avidya* has *maya*, *prakriti*, *avyakta*, *avyakrita*, *tamas*, and *shakti* as synonyms.

- *Avidya* functions at the individual level and *maya* at the cosmic level.

- Cosmic *avidya* (*maya*) is one, while individual *avidya* is manifold.

- *Brahman* is the locus of cosmic *avidya* (*maya*) and *jiva* the locus of individual *avidya*.

- *Avidya* has as its object *Brahman*.

- Both *Brahman* and *maya* are the material (*upadana*) cause of the world. However, *Brahman* is the illusory or apparent material cause, while *maya* is the real or the transforming material cause.

- *Jiva*-s are *pratibimba*-s, reflections of *Brahman* in *antahkarana* (internal organ). The reflected images have no reality other than that of the original *bimba* (*Brahman*). This doctrine is called *pratibimba-vada* (the doctrine of reflection).

• *Shravana* (hearing) is the main factor in Realization, while *manana* (reflection) and *nididhyasana* (deep meditation) are auxiliaries.

• *Moksha* is attained simultaneously with *jnana* and the continuance of the body does not impose any limitation. Hence, *jivan-mukti* (liberation while alive) is recognized as true Liberation.

Bhamati Prasthana is at present the second most important school of Advaita. It was established by Vacaspati Misra (9th century A.D.) and the name of the school comes from his celebrated work *Bhamati*, a commentary on Shankara's *Brahma Sutra Bhashya*.

Some of the principal works that define the Bhamati School are:

• *Bhamati* ~ Vacaspati Misra
• *Kalpataru* ~ Amalananda
• *Parimala* ~ Appayya Dikshita
• *Bhamati Tilaka* ~ Allala Suri
• *Bhamati Vyakhya* ~ Sriranganatha

The principal tenets of the Bhamati School are:

• *Jiva* is the locus of both cosmic *avidya* (*maya*) and individual *avidya*. *Brahman*, being of the nature of *vidya* (knowledge), cannot be the locus of *avidya*.

• *Avidya* has as its object *Brahman*.

• *Avidya* is different in each *jiva* and is therefore manifold.

• *Avidya* possesses only the veiling power (*avarana-shakti*).

• *Avidya* is the efficient (*nimitta*) cause of the world in the capacity of being an error.

• *Brahman* is the material (*upadana*) cause of the world. It is also the efficient (*nimitta*) cause, but here *Brahman* is *Ishvara* – *Brahman* particularized as the object of *avidya*.

• *Maya* and *avidya* are only the accessory (*sahakarin*) cause of the world.

• There are two types of *avidya*: *mulavidya* or *karanavidya* (primal nescience) and *tulavidya* or *karyavidya* (resultant nescience). The latter is responsible for *bhramasamskara*-s (error impressions). Resultant individual nescience is removed by cognition of the true or real object; while primal nescience is destroyed only by the realization of its object, *Brahman*.

• *Jiva*-s are appearances of *Brahman* being limited by *avidya*. Just as a pot limits infinite space, individual *avidya* limits *Brahman* and makes it appear as *jiva*-s. This doctrine is called *avaccheda-vada* (the doctrine of limitation).

• *Nididhyasana* (deep meditation) is the main factor in Realization, while *shravana* (hearing) and *manana* (reflection) are subsidiaries.

• *Moksha* is not attained simultaneously with *jnana*, for the continuance of the body imposes limitation, implying the existence of a trace of *avidya*. Only the death of the body puts an end to this trace and confers liberation. Hence, only *videha-mukti* (liberation after death) is admitted as true Liberation.

Varttika Prasthana is the third school of Advaita and was promoted by Sureshvara (8th century A.D.), one of the four disciples of Shankara, and by Sarvajnatma (8th century A.D.). The Varttika School gets its name from Sureshvara's famous works *varttika*-s (critiques on philosophical commentaries).

ॐ

Though, initially it was the most important of the Advaitic schools, in time it lost its authority and was overshadowed by the more successful Vivarana School. From their inceptions, both schools shared common views and doctrines but also had their differences.

The Varttika School is defined by the following major works:

- *Brihadaranyaka Bhashya Varttika* ~ Sureshvara
- *Taittiriya Bhashya Varttika* ~ Sureshvara
- *Naishkarmya Siddhi* ~ Sureshvara
- *Samkshepa Shariraka* ~ Sarvajnatma
- *Chandrika* ~ Jnanottama
- *Bhava Tattvaprakasika* ~ Chitsukha

The principal tenets of the Varttika School are:

- *Avidya* is one only and pervades all *jiva*-s.

- *Avidya* possesses twofold power: veiling (*avarana-shakti*) and projecting (*vikshepa-shakti*).

- *Brahman* is the locus of *avidya*.

- *Avidya* has as its object *Brahman*.

- *Brahman* and *maya* are the material (*upadana*) cause of the world. *Brahman* is the primal or direct cause and *maya* is the secondary or mediate cause.

- *Jiva*-s are but *abhasa*-s or false appearances of *Brahman* in the individual mind. This doctrine is called *abhasa-vada* (the doctrine of false appearance).

- *Shravana* (hearing) of the *mahavakya*-s (great sentences) can produce immediate cognition of *Brahman*, and thus it is the

ॐ

main factor in Realization. *Manana* (reflection) and *nididhyasana* (deep meditation) are auxiliaries.

• *Moksha* is attained simultaneously with *jnana*, and the continuance of the body does not impose any limitation. Hence, only *jivan-mukti* (liberation while alive) is accepted as true Liberation.

The differences between the three schools of Advaita are not between the fundamental Advaitic principles, but rather differences of approach and interpretation of them. Though all schools offer excellent doctrines and answers regarding the nature of *Brahman* and other important topics, each school has its own logical problems which remain unresolved.

Many authors and commentators do not belong strictly to any one of the three schools of Advaita, among these are: Jnanaghana, Jnanottama, Vimuktatman, Sriharsha, and Chitsukha.

Sannyasa Order

Beginning with Shankara two important traditions in Advaita emerged and continue to this day. On the one hand, there is the philosophical tradition of the large number of Advaitic works, and on the other hand, there is the religious tradition of the *Dasanami Sampradaya* (lineage of monks), which is rooted in the *Upanishad*-s and Shankara's works.

The two aspects of Advaita Vedanta are well related to each other, as most of the famous authors in the philosophical tradition were monks belonging to the Shankara Order or *Dasanami Sampradaya*. And too, both aspects of the tradition share the same doctrines, morals, and positions with regard to the ultimate goal of life.

Shankara organized the *Dasanami Sampradaya* and established four *matha*-s (monasteries) in India; one *matha* each in the North, South, East, and West. The succeeding heads of the Advaita *matha*-s bear the title *Shankaracharya*-s, taken after the name of the founder. Shankara is usually called Adi Shankara, which means the first *Shankaracharya*, distinguishing him from his four disciples and their successors.

The four *matha*-s established by Shankara are known in the Advaitic tradition as the *amnaya matha*-s and each of these *matha*-s has allocated one of the four *Veda*-s. The order organized by Shankara, *Dasanami*, means ten (*dasa*) names (*nama*) and these names are added as suffixes to the names of all *sannyasin*-s who followed after Shankara. Traditionally, the ten *dasanami* suffixes are distributed among the four *amnaya matha*-s as follows:

(1) *Jyoti Matha*, located in North India (Badrinath, Uttaranchal State), is associated with *Atharva Veda* and has allocated three suffixes, *Sagara, Parvata*, and *Giri*.

(2) *Shringeri Matha*, located in South India (Sringeri, Karnataka State), is associated with *Yajur Veda* and has allocated three suffixes, *Puri, Bharati*, and *Sarasvati*.

(3) *Govardhana Matha*, located in East India (Puri, Orissa State), is associated with *Rig Veda* and has allocated two suffixes, *Vana* and *Aranya*.

(4) *Sharada Matha*, located in West India (Dvarka, Gujarat State), is associated with *Sama Veda* and has allocated two suffixes, *Tirtha and Ashrama*.

Among these ten suffixes, *Aranya, Ashrama, Parvata, Vana*, and *Sagara* are rarely encountered nowadays.

In addition to the above mentioned *matha*-s another *matha, Kamakothi* in Kanchipuram (Tamil Nadu State), is well-known and usually considered as important as the four main *matha*-s.

Many notable post-Shankara authors were heads of the four main *matha*-s. *Shringeri* is the only *matha* which has had an unbroken line of succession from Shankara. The other three *matha*-s have had the succession interrupted at one time or another, for different reasons. The longest break in the line of succession was in the case of *Jyoti Matha*, where the seat lay vacant for about 165 years. Traditionally each *Shankaracharya* should nominate his successor. All over India *Shankaracharya*-s are held in high respect by almost all Hindu sects. The *matha*-s in India operate quite independently of one another and do not interfere with each other unless necessary.

Dasanami sannyasin-s typically wear ochre-colored robes and carry on their shoulders a tiger or panther skin to sit on. They wear a mark (*tilaka*), made with ash from ritualistic fires, consisting of three horizontal bands across the forehead and on other parts of the body. They have their heads and beards clean shaven and wear a *mala* consisting of 108 *rudraksha* seeds. All *dasanami* monks belong to the tradition of *ekadandi sannyasa*, which means they carry a single bamboo stick, representing the identity between *Atman* and *Brahman*.

Dasanami Sampradaya is not a *Shaiva* sect and *dasanami sannyasin*-s are not exclusively *Shaiva* ascetics. However, usually they do worship both *Shiva* and *Vishnu* and also other deities, like *Shakti*, *Ganesha*, *Lakshmi*, etc. From a philosophical point of view, Advaita opposes the *Vaishnava* (theistic and dualistic) schools of Vedanta, as well as the *Shaiva Siddhanta* (realistic and dualistic) and *Shaiva Kashmira* (idealistic and monistic). Yet, by emphasizing *sannyasa* (renunciation) and considering Lord Shiva as the archetype of the ascetic, Advaita *Sampradaya* has more in common with the *Shaiva* tradition than with the *Vaishnava* tradition. Additionally, it has more in common with the *Shaiva* schools because they are more non-dualistic than the *Vaishnava*.

Besides the well-known traditional Advaita *matha*-s, in the last century, various *Sannyasin*-s of the *Dasanami* Order have established a number of other modern spiritual organizations. Such institutions usually teach more or less pure Advaita Vedanta, though some of them combine it with the Yoga System or other beliefs or systems, and some others consider activities like social service very important.

The best known of the modern organizations are: the Ramakrishna Mission (Ramakrishna Paramahamsa), Vedanta Society (Svami Vivekananda), Self-Realization Fellowship (Paramahamsa Yogananda), Divine Life Society (Svami

Sivananda), and Chinmaya Mission (Svami Chinmayananda). The founders are linked to one or another of the four *matha*: Ramakrishna Paramahamsa and Svami Vivekananda are linked to Govardhana Matha (Puri), Paramahamsa Yogananda to *Jyoti Matha* (Badrinath), Svami Sivananda and Svami Chinmayananda to *Shringeri Matha* (Sringeri).

Though a great number of famous or completely anonymous sages and saints have merged into the non-dual *Brahman*, realizing the highest Advaitic truth, many of them have been completely independent of the *Dasanami* Order. These realized souls are known as *atyashrami*-s and are classed as beyond *sannyasin*-s. Within the last century two great souls can be mentioned as examples. One is the great sage of Arunachala, Sri Bhagavan Ramana Maharshi (1879-1950), who never took formal *sannyasa* but was the embodiment of pure Advaitic spirit and a great *jivan-mukta*. The second is the famous saint, Sri Anandamayi Ma of Haridvar (1896-1982), who attained realization without a *guru* or study of the sacred scriptures.

"*No living being whatsoever is born; there is no becoming for it. This is that highest truth where nothing whatsoever is born.*"

To the question – does the world of duality, which is comprised of sentient and insentient phenomena, appear before us and what will its fate be – the answer provided by Gaudapada in the first part of *Mandukya Karika* (*AgamaPrakarana*, verse 18) is:

"*If the multiplicity were imagined, it would vanish. Such doctrine is merely for the purpose of instruction. When known, duality ceases to exist.*"

The answer is further supplemented with a verse from the second part (*Vaitathya Prakarana*, verse 34):

"*From the standpoint of the Self the world does not exist; nor does it exist as independent, neither differentiated nor non-differentiated. This is what the wise knows.*"

Gaudapada investigates various theories of creation and rejects them all. Some say that creation is the expansion (*vibhuti*) of *Brahman*. Others say that it is like a dream (*svapna*) or an illusion (*maya*). Some believe that it is the will (*ichcha*) of *Brahman*. Those who believe in time state that creation proceeds from time (*kala*). Still others say that creation is an act of enjoyment (*bhoga*). And some say that it is the sport (*krida*) of *Brahman*. But Gaudapada finds all these theories of creation unacceptable and declares that for *Brahman*, being the Full (*purna*), there can be no gain, loss, or division, for any reason whatsoever.

Gaudapada firmly states that *ajati-vada* is rooted in the *Upanishad*-s, which clearly, repeatedly, and definitively declare that the ultimate reality is *Brahman* which is non-dual, self-known, self-evident, and eternal; while difference, duality, plurality, and origination is nothing but mere appearance:

ॐ

Ajati Vada

The doctrine that states that *Atman* is, in the absolute sense, *janmadivikararahita* (devoid of changes or mutations like birth, growth, death, etc.) and also *prapanchopashama* (devoid of the world of multiplicity), is called *ajati-vada* in Advaitic parlance. *Ajati-vada* (doctrine of non-origination or no-creation) was advocated by Acharya Gaudapada in his great *Karika* (explanatory treatise) on the *Mandukya Upanishad*.

The outstanding doctrine of *ajati-vada* is encapsulated in the famous and striking verse found in the second part of *Mandukya Karika* (*Vaitathya Prakarana*, verse 32):

"There is no dissolution, no birth, none in bondage and none aspiring for wisdom, no seeker of liberation and none liberated. This is the Absolute Truth."

Other key verses pointing to the same ultimate truth (*paramartika-satya*) are found in *Advaita Prakarana*, verse 33:

"They assert the knowledge free from imagination, birthless, not different from what is known. Brahman is that which is known, birthless, eternal. The birthless knows the birthless."

And furthermore in *Alatashanti Prakarana*, verse 71:

- *"There is no second to Atman"* (*Brihadaranyaka Upanishad,* IV, 3, 23).

- *"Brahman is one without a second"* (*Chandogya Upanishad,* VI, 2,2).

- *"This self is Brahman "* (*Brihadaranyaka Upanishad,* II, 5, 19).

- *"How can delusion and suffering touch him who sees the non-dual Self everywhere"* (*Isavashya Upanishad,* 7).

- *"The knower of Brahman becomes Brahman "* (*Mundaka Upanishad,* III, 2, 9).

- *"He goes from death to death who sees any difference here. "* (*Katha Upanishad,* II, 1, 10).

- *"He goes from death to death who sees multiplicity in It. This, verily, is That."* (*Katha Upanishad,* II, 1, 11).

- *"In utter darkness are those who worship the creation "* (*Isavashya Upanishad,* 12).

These statements of the *Upanishad*-s agree in teaching the non-dual reality of Advaita by proclaiming and praising the non-difference between *jiva,* *Atman,* and *Brahman.*

Not only by the authority of scriptures but also by independent reasoning, says Gaudapada, *ajati-vada* can be proved. Thus, in his exposition of Advaita he guides the seeker with many arguments, step by step, to the Supreme Truth – that nothing whatsoever is born or created.

No-creation (*ajati*) implies that causality is an illusion. But for whom is it an illusion? It is for him who has realized the truth of non-duality. From the standpoint of those who take the pluralistic universe to be real, the world and its changes, the soul and its states, cannot be easily and completely dismissed. Nevertheless, before one undertakes enquiry into the Truth, one should at least understand theoretically that the dualistic world, though it appears, cannot be real.

The seeker who has understood the Advaitic teaching will realize that the question of cause never arises. The consideration of *maya* and *avidya* is only a temporary compromise for the immature seeker to satisfy his longing for an explanation of the world. In every individual case the presence of *avidya* can be traced to the absence of enquiry into the Self or Truth. The doctrine of *maya* and *avidya* is offered only to help the aspirant to rise to the plane of absolute oneness.

It should be remembered that from the Absolute point of view (*paramarthika-satya*) *Brahman* neither creates nor destroys, He only is. Thus, according to *Mandukya Karika*, the *Upanishad*-s, and other ancient Advaitic texts, the final truth regarding *Brahman* and creation is that *Brahman* is Birthless (*aja*), in the sense that it is the ever existent, and that creation is "birthless" (*aja*) as well, but in the opposite sense, that it never really exists.

Conclusion

After reading the introductory part of this book, it is important that the reader understand that Advaita accomplishes its purpose when it has proved the existence of the non-dual Absolute Truth, which resolves everything into Itself. And if there is genuine understanding of this Advaitic Truth and doctrine, then what awaits the aspirant is Self-Realization.

Though, the Advaitic teaching has never been one which could be addressed to the masses, still, this outstanding philosophy, since the time of Gaudapada and Shankara and to this day, has attracted a good number of true followers all over the world, making a distinguished contribution to the spiritual tradition of mankind.

If Advaitic philosophy is not popular among a large number of spiritual seekers, the main reason could be the direct and radical method it employs to establish the Truth. While the idea that all is *Brahman* appears exciting and encouraging, the statement that the world is false or illusion is dry and disturbing. The negation of the world is just too much for inexperienced seekers And their reactions and worries are understandable, taking into account that Advaita is a first-class means to Liberation and is meant for advanced aspirants.

When the aspirant is ripe he certainly will be able to reflect upon the nature of the world and realize that he is nothing but the witness of a universal and extraordinary drama, a play of shadows in the shape of states, where the actors and the scenes are but the expression of the Self, without loss of Oneness. As long as he takes shadow as reality, he is trapped in joys and sorrows, in births and deaths. But, when he knows that they are merely shadows and that Reality can project no shadow, then the cosmic show deludes him no longer. States, arising and fading, fool him no more. And finally, he recognizes himself as the changeless *Brahman*, who only apparently projects, preserves, and removes the whole phenomenal spectacle . . . leaving behind no trace . . . of it all.

PART TWO

Advaita Wisdom

Upanishads

Mandukya Upanishad

1. This letter that is *OM* is all this. Of this a clear exposition (is started with). All that is past, present or future is verily *OM*. And whatever is beyond the three periods of time is also verily *OM*.

❀ ❀ ❀

2. All this is surely *Brahman*. This Self is *Brahman*. The Self as It is, is possessed of four quarters.

❀ ❀ ❀

3. The first quarter is *Vaishvanara* whose sphere (of action) is the waking state, whose consciousness relates to external things, who is possessed of seven limbs and nineteen mouths, and who enjoys gross things.

❀ ❀ ❀

4. *Taijasa* is the second quarter, whose sphere (of action) is the dream state, whose consciousness is internal, who is possessed of seven limbs and nineteen mouths, and who enjoys subtle objects

5. That state is deep sleep where the sleeper does not desire any enjoyable thing and does not see any dream. The third quarter is *Prajna* who has deep sleep as his sphere, in whom everything becomes undifferentiated, who is a mass of mere consciousness, who abounds in bliss, who is surely an enjoyer of bliss, and who is the doorway to the experience (of the dream and waking states).

❁   ❁   ❁

6. This one is the Lord of all; this one is Omniscient; this one is the inner Director (of all); this one is the Source of all; this one is verily the place of origin and dissolution of all beings.

❁   ❁   ❁

7. They consider the fourth to be that which is not conscious of the internal world, nor conscious of the external world, nor conscious of both the worlds, nor a mass of consciousness, nor conscious, nor unconscious; which is unseen, beyond empirical dealings, beyond the grasp (of the organs of action), uninferable, unthinkable, and indescribable; whose valid proof consists in the single belief in the Self; in which all phenomena cease; and which is unchanging, auspicious, and non-dual. That is the Self, and That is to be known.

❁   ❁   ❁

8. That very Self, considered from the standpoint of the syllable (denoting It) is *OM*. Considered from the standpoint of the letters (constituting *OM*), the quarters (of the Self) are the letters (of *OM*) and the letters are the quarters. (The letters are): *A, U, and M.*

❁   ❁   ❁

9. *Vaishvanara,* having the waking state as his sphere, is the first letter *A,* because of (the similarity of) pervasiveness of being the first. He who knows thus, does verily attain all desirable things, and becomes the foremost.

🕉

10. He who is *Taijasa* with the state of dream as his sphere (of activity) is the second letter *U* (of *OM*); because of the similarity of excellence and intermediateness. He who knows thus increases the current of knowledge and becomes equal to all. None is born in his line who is not a knower of *Brahman*.

❂ ❂ ❂

11. *Prajna* with his sphere of activity in the sleep state is *M*, the third letter of *OM*, because of measuring or because of absorption. Anyone who knows thus measures all this, and he becomes the place of absorption.

❂ ❂ ❂

12. The partless *OM* is *Turiya* – beyond all conventional dealings, the limit of the negation of the phenomenal world, the auspicious and the non-dual. *OM* is thus the Self to be sure. He who knows thus enters the Self through his self.

❂ ❂ ❂

Brihadaranyaka Upanishad

I.4.10. This self was indeed *Brahman* in the beginning. It knew itself only as "I am *Brahman*". Therefore, it became all. And whoever among the gods had this enlightenment, also became that *Brahman*. It is the same with the seers (*rishi*-s), the same with men. The seer Vamadeva, having realized this self as That, came to know: "I was Manu and the sun". And to this day, whoever in a like manner knows the self as "I am *Brahman*", becomes all this universe. Even the gods cannot prevent his becoming this, for he has become their Self.

ॐ

Now, if a man worships another deity, thinking: "He is one and I am another," he does not know. He is like an animal to the gods. As many animals serve a man, so does each man serve the gods. Even if one animal is taken away, it causes anguish to the owner; how much more so when many are taken away! Therefore it is not pleasing to the gods that men should know this.

❊   ❊   ❊

II.3.1. Verily, there are two forms of *Brahman*: gross and subtle, mortal and immortal, limited and unlimited, definite and indefinite.

❊   ❊   ❊

II.3.6. ...Now therefore, the description of *Brahman*: "Not this, not this" (*neti, neti*); for there is no other and more appropriate description than this "Not this." Now the designation of *Brahman*: "The Truth of truth". The vital breath is truth and It (*Brahman*) is the Truth of that.

❊   ❊   ❊

II.4.6. The Brahmin rejects one who knows him as different from the Self. The *Kshatriya* rejects one who knows him as different from the Self. The worlds reject one who knows them as different from the Self. The gods reject one who knows them as different from the Self. The beings reject one who knows them as different from the Self. The All rejects one who knows it as different from the Self. This Brahmin, this *Kshatriya*, these worlds, these gods, these beings, and this All – are that Self.

❊   ❊   ❊

II.4.12. "As a lump of salt dropped into water becomes dissolved in water and cannot be taken out again, but wherever we taste the water it tastes salt, even so, my dear, this

🕉

great, endless, infinite Reality is Pure Intelligence alone. This self comes out as a separate entity from these elements and with their destruction, this separate existence also is destroyed. After attaining oneness it has no more consciousness. This is what I say, my dear.

❁ ❁ ❁

II.4.14. For, where there is duality, as it were, then one smells another, then one sees another, then one hears another, then one addresses another, then one thinks of another, then one knows another; but where all has become the very Self of the Knower of *Brahman*, whom and through what would one see, then whom and through what would one hear, then whom and through what would one think, then whom and through what would one know? Through what would one know That through which one knows everything here? Lo! Through what would one know the Knower?

❁ ❁ ❁

III.4.2. Ushasta, the son of Chakra, said: "You have explained it as one might say 'Such is a cow', 'Such is a horse'. Tell me precisely the Brahman that is immediate and direct – the self that is within all."
"This is your self that is within all."
"Which is within all, Yajnavalkya?"
"You cannot see the seer of seeing; you cannot hear the hearer of hearing; you cannot think of the thinker of thinking; you cannot know the knower of knowing. This is your self that is within all; everything else but this is perishable."
Thereupon Ushasta, the son of Chakra, held his peace.

❁ ❁ ❁

III.5.1. Next Kahola, the son of Kushitaka, questioned him. "Yajnavalkya," said he, "explain to me the Brahman that is directly and immediately perceived – the self that is within all."

ॐ

"This is your self that is within all."

"Which self is within all, Yajnavalkya?"

"It is that which transcends hunger and thirst, grief, delusion, old age and death. Having realized this Self, Brahmins give up the desire for sons, the desire for wealth, and the desire for the worlds and lead the life of religious mendicants. That which is the desire for sons is the desire for wealth and that which is the desire for wealth is the desire for the worlds; for both these are but desires.

Therefore, a Brahmin, after he is done with scholarship, should try to live on that strength which comes of scholarship. After he is done with that strength and scholarship, he becomes meditative and after he is done with both meditativeness and non-meditativeness, he becomes a knower of Brahman.

How does the knower of Brahman behave? Howsoever he may behave he is such indeed. Everything else but this is perishable."

❁   ❁   ❁

III.7.4. "He who inhabits water, yet is within water, whom water does not know, whose body water is and who controls water from within. He is your Self, the Inner Controller, the Immortal."

❁   ❁   ❁

III.7.5. "He who inhabits fire, yet is within fire, whom fire does not know, whose body fire is and who controls fire from within. He is your Self, the Inner Controller, the Immortal."

❁   ❁   ❁

III.7.6. "He who inhabits the sky, yet is within the sky, whom the sky does not know, whose body the sky is and who controls the sky from within. He is your Self, the Inner Controller, the Immortal."

III.7.7. "He who inhabits the air, yet is within the air, whom the air does not know, whose body the air is and who controls the air from within. He is your Self, the Inner Controller, the Immortal."

❁ ❁ ❁

III.7.8. "He who inhabits heaven, yet is within heaven, whom heaven does not know, whose body heaven is and who controls heaven from within. He is your Self, the Inner Controller, the Immortal."

❁ ❁ ❁

III.7.9. "He who inhabits the sun, yet is within the sun, whom the sun does not know, whose body the sun is and who controls the sun from within. He is your Self, the Inner Controller, the Immortal."

❁ ❁ ❁

III.7.10. "He who inhabits the quarters of space, yet is within them, whom the quarters do not know, whose body the quarters are and who controls the quarters from within. He is your Self, the Inner Controller, the Immortal."

❁ ❁ ❁

III.7.11. "He who inhabits the moon and stars, yet is within the moon and stars, whom the moon and stars do not know, whose body the moon and stars are and who controls the moon and stars from within. He is your Self, the Inner Controller, the Immortal."

❁ ❁ ❁

III.7.12. "He who inhabits the *akasha*, yet is within the *akasha*, whom the *akasha* does not know, whose body the *akasha* is and who controls the *akasha* from within. He is your Self, the Inner Controller, the Immortal."

III.7.13. "He who inhabits darkness, yet is within darkness, whom darkness does not know, whose body darkness is and who controls darkness from within. He is your Self, the Inner Controller, the Immortal."

✿   ✿   ✿

III.7.14. "He who inhabits light, yet is within light, whom light does not know, whose body light is and who controls light from within. He is your Self, the Inner Controller, the Immortal."

✿   ✿   ✿

III.7.23. ..."He is never seen, but is the Seer; He is never heard, but is the Hearer; He is never thought of, but is the Thinker; He is never known, but is the Knower. There is no other seer than He, there is no other hearer than He, there is no other thinker than He, there is no other knower than He. He is your Self, the Inner Controller, the Immortal. Everything else but Him is perishable."

✿   ✿   ✿

III.8.8. He said: "That, O Gargi, the knowers of *Brahman* call the Imperishable. It is neither gross nor subtle, neither short nor long, neither red nor moist; It is neither shadow nor darkness, neither air nor *akasha*; It is unattached; It is without taste or smell, without eyes or ears, without tongue or mind; It is non-effulgent, without vital breath or mouth, without measure and without exterior or interior. It does not eat anything, nor is It eaten by anyone."

✿   ✿   ✿

III.8.11. "Verily, that Imperishable, O Gargi, is never seen but is the Seer; It is never heard, but is the Hearer; It is never thought of, but is the Thinker; It is never known, but is the Knower. There is no other seer but This, there is no other hearer but

ॐ

This, there is no other thinker but This, there is no other knower but This. By this imperishable, O Gargi, is the unmanifested *akasha* pervaded."

❀ ❀ ❀

IV.2.4. "...This self is That which has been described as 'Not this, not this'. It is imperceptible, for It is never perceived; undecaying, for It never decays; unattached, for It is never attached; unfettered, for It never feels pain and never suffers injury."

"Verily, O Janaka, you have attained That which is free from fear," said Yajnavalkya.

"Venerable Yajnavalkya," said Emperor Janaka, "may that fearless *Brahman* be yours too, for you have made known to us the fearless *Brahman*. Salutations to you! Here is the Empire of Videha and also myself at your service."

❀ ❀ ❀

IV.3.2. "Yajnavalkya, what serves as light for a man?"

"The light of the sun, O Emperor", said Yajnavalkya, "for with the sun as light he sits, goes out, works and returns."

"Just so, Yajnavalkya."

❀ ❀ ❀

IV.3.3. "When the sun has set, Yajnavalkya, what serves as light for a man?"

"The moon serves as his light, for with the moon as light he sits, goes out, works and returns."

"Just so, Yajnavalkya."

❀ ❀ ❀

IV.3.4. "When the sun has set and the moon has set, Yajnavalkya, what serves as light for a man?"

"Fire serves as his light, for with fire as light he sits, goes out, works and returns."

"Just so, Yajnavalkya."

ॐ

IV.3.5. "When the sun has set, Yajnavalkya and the moon has set and the fire has gone out, what serves as light for a man?" "Speech (sound) serves as his light, for with speech as light he sits, goes out, works and returns. Therefore, Your Majesty, when one cannot see even one's own hand, yet when a sound is uttered, one can go there."
"Just so, Yajnavalkya."

✿   ✿   ✿

IV.3.6. "When the sun has set, Yajnavalkya and the moon has set and the fire has gone out and speech has stopped, what serves as light for a man?"
"The Self, indeed, is his light, for with the Self as light he sits, goes out, works and returns."

✿   ✿   ✿

IV.3.30. "And when it appears that in deep sleep it does not know, yet it is knowing though it does not know; for there is no cessation of the knowing of the knower, because the knower is imperishable. There is then, however, no second thing separate from the knower that it could know."

✿   ✿   ✿

IV.3.33. "If a person is perfect of body and is prosperous, lord of others and most lavishly supplied with all human enjoyments, he represents the highest blessing among men. This human bliss multiplied a hundred times makes one measure of the bliss of the Manes who have won their own world. The bliss of these Manes who have won their world, multiplied a hundred times, makes one measure of bliss in the world of the *gandharva*-s. The bliss of the *gandharva*-s, multiplied a hundred times, makes one measure of the bliss of the gods by action (those who attain godhood through sacrificial rites). The bliss of the gods by action, multiplied a hundred times, makes one measure of the bliss of the gods by birth, as also of one who is versed in the *Veda*-s, sinless and free from desire. The bliss of the gods by birth, multiplied a hundred times, makes one measure of bliss in the World of *Prajapan* (*Viraj*), as also of one who is versed in the *Veda*-s, sinless and free from desire. The bliss in the World of *Prajapati*, multiplied a hundred times, makes one measure of bliss in the World of *Brahma* (*Hiranyagarbha*), as also of one who is versed in the *Veda*-s, sinless and free from desire. This, indeed, is the supreme bliss. This is the state of *Brahman*, O Emperor," said Yajnavalkya.

❀ ❀ ❀

IV.4.19. Through the mind alone is *Brahman* to be realized. There is in It no diversity. He goes from death to death who sees in It, as it were, diversity.

❀ ❀ ❀

IV.4.20. Unknowable and constant, It should be realized in one form only. The Self is free from taint, beyond the *akasha*, birthless, infinite and unchanging.

❀ ❀ ❀

IV.4.21. The intelligent seeker of *Brahman*, learning about the Self alone, should practice wisdom (*prajna*). Let him not think of too many words, for that is exhausting to the organ of speech.

❀ ❀ ❀

IV.4.22. ...The knowers of *Brahman* of olden times, it is said, did not wish for offspring because they thought: "What shall we do with offspring – we who have attained this Self, this World?" They gave up, it is said, their desire for sons, for wealth and for the worlds and led the life of religious mendicants. That which is the desire for sons is the desire for wealth and that which is

🕉

the desire for wealth is the desire for the worlds; for both these, indeed, are but desires.

This Self is That which has been described as "not this, not this". It is imperceptible, for It is not perceived; undecaying, for It never decays; unattached, for It is never attached; unfettered, for It never feels pain and never suffers injury.

Him who knows this, these two thoughts do not overcome: "For this I did an evil deed and for this I did a good deed." He overcomes both. Things done or not done do not afflict him.

❖ ❖ ❖

IV.4.25. That great, unborn Self is undecaying, immortal, undying, fearless; It is *Brahman* (infinite). *Brahman* is indeed fearless. He who knows It as such becomes the fearless *Brahman*.

❖ ❖ ❖

IV.5.6. And he said: "Verily, not for the sake of the husband, my dear, is the husband loved, but he is loved for the sake of the self which, in its true nature, is one with the Supreme Self."

"Verily, not for the sake of the wife, my dear, is the wife loved, but she is loved for the sake of the self."

"Verily, not for the sake of the sons, my dear, are the sons loved, but they are loved for the sake of the self."

"Verily, not for the sake of wealth, my dear, is wealth loved, but it is loved for the sake of the self."

"Verily, not for the sake of the animals, my dear, are the animals loved, but they are loved for the sake of the self."

"Verily, not for the sake of the Brahmin, my dear, is the Brahmin loved, but he is loved for the sake of the self."

"Verily, not for the sake of the *Kshatriya*, my dear, is the *Kshatriya* loved, but he is loved for the sake of the self."

"Verily, not for the sake of the worlds, my dear, are the worlds loved, but they are loved for the sake of the self."

"Verily, not for the sake of the gods, my dear, are the gods loved, but they are loved for the sake of the self."

"Verily, not for the sake of the *Veda*-s, my dear, are the *Veda*-s loved, but they are loved for the sake of the self."

"Verily, not for the sake of the beings, my dear, are the beings loved, but they are loved for the sake of the self."

"Verily, not for the sake of the All, my dear, is the All loved, but it is loved for the sake of the self."

"Verily, my dear Maitreyi, it is the Self that should be realized – should be heard of, reflected on and meditated upon. By the realization of the Self, my dear, through hearing, reflection and meditation, all this is known."

✿   ✿   ✿

IV.5.15. "For when there is duality, as it were, then one sees another, one smells another, one tastes another, one speaks to another, one hears another, one thinks of another, one touches another, one knows another. But when to the knower of *Brahman* everything has become the Self, then what should he see and through what, what should he smell and through what, what should he taste and through what, what should he speak and through what, what should he hear and through what, what should he think and through what, what should he touch and through what, what should he know and through what? Through what should one know That owing to which all this is known?"

"This Self is That which has been described as 'Not this, not this.' It is imperceptible, for It is never perceived; undecaying, for It never decays; unattached, for It never attaches Itself; unfettered, for It never feels pain and never suffers injury. Through what, O Maitreyi, should one know the Knower?"

"Thus you have the instruction given to you. This much, indeed, is the means to Immortality."

Having said this, Yajnavalkya renounced home.

VII.1.1. *OM*. Infinite is That *Brahman*, infinite in this manifested universe. From the Infinite *Brahman* proceeds the infinite. After the realization of the Great Identity, when the infinity of the infinite universe merges in the Infinite *Brahman*, there remains the Infinite *Brahman* alone.

✿   ✿   ✿

Chandogya Upanishad

III.14.1. All this is *Brahman*. From It the universe comes forth, in It the universe merges and in It the universe breathes. Therefore a man should meditate on *Brahman* with a calm mind.

Now, verily, a man consists of will. As he wills in this world, so does he become when he has departed hence. Let him with this knowledge in mind form his will.

✿   ✿   ✿

VI.2.1. "In the beginning my dear, this universe was Being (*Sat*) alone, one only without a second. Some say that in the beginning this was non-being (*asat*) alone, one only without a second; and from that non-being, Being was born."

✿   ✿   ✿

VI.2.2. Aruni said: "But how, indeed, could it be thus, my dear? How could Being be born from non-being? No, my dear, it was Being alone that existed in the beginning, one only without a second."

✿   ✿   ✿

VI.2.3. "It (Being, or *Brahman*) thought: 'May I be many; may I grow forth.' It created fire. That fire thought: 'May I be many;

may I grow forth.' It created water. That is why, whenever a person is hot and perspires, water is produced from fire (heat) alone."

❀   ❀   ❀

VI.8.7. "Now, that which is the subtle essence – in it all that exists has its self. That is the True. That is the Self. That thou art, Svetaketu." "Please, venerable Sir, give me further instruction", said the son. "So be it, my dear", the father replied.

❀   ❀   ❀

VI.9.1-2. "As bees, my dear, make honey by collecting the juices of trees located at different places, and reduce them to one form, and as these juices have no discrimination so as to be able to say: 'I am the juice of this tree', or 'I am the juice of that tree' – even so, indeed, my dear, all these creatures, though they reach Pure Being, do not know that they have reached Pure Being."

❀   ❀   ❀

VI.13.1. "After keeping this salt in the water, then come to me in the morning." He did accordingly. To him he said, "O dear one, fetch that salt which you kept in the water at night." He could not find it after searching.

❀   ❀   ❀

VI.13.2. "O dear one (you do not perceive it), remaining dissolved as it does. Now, if you want to perceive it sip from its top. How does it taste?"
"It is salty."
"Sip from the middle. How does it taste?"
"It is salty."
"Sip from the bottom. How does it taste?"
"It is salty."
"Throwing this away, come to me."

ॐ

With regard to that, he acted in that way and said, "That (salt) exists always."

To him, he (the father) said, "O good-looking one, you cannot perceive Existence though it is verily present here itself. Surely it is here."

❀ ❀ ❀

VI.13.3. "That which is this subtle essence, all this has got That as the Self. That is Truth. That is the Self. Thou art That, O Svetaketu."

❀ ❀ ❀

VII.1.1. *OM*. Narada approached Sanatkumara saying, "Teach me, O venerable sir."

To him he said: "You approach me with that which you know. I shall tell you of things that are beyond them."

❀ ❀ ❀

VII.1.2. "O venerable sir, I read the *Rig-Veda, Yajur-Veda, Sama-Veda* and *Atharva-Veda* the fourth. History and mythology which are the fifth *Veda*, grammar, the rites for the Manes, mathematics, the subject of natural disturbances, mineralogy, logic, ethics, etymology, the subject of ancillary knowledge concerning the *Veda*-s, the science of the elements, the science of archery, astronomy, the science of serpents, the subject of fine arts – I know all these, O venerable sir!"

❀ ❀ ❀

VII.1.3. "O venerable sir, such as I am, I merely know the subjects textually. But I am not a knower of the Self. It has been heard by me, from venerable people like you, that a knower of the Self goes beyond sorrow. Such as I am, I am full of sorrow. O venerable sir, please take me beyond sorrow."

To him he said: "All these, whatsoever that you have learnt are merely names."

🕉

VII.23.1. "That which indeed is the Infinite, that is joy. There is no joy in the finite. The Infinite alone is joy."

✿   ✿   ✿

VII.24.1. "The Infinite is that where one does not see anything else, does not hear anything else, does not understand anything else. Hence the finite is that where one sees something else, hears something else and understands something else. That which indeed is the Infinite is immortal. On the other hand, that which is finite is mortal."

✿   ✿   ✿

VII.25.1. "That Infinite, indeed, is below. It is above. It is behind. It is before. It is to the south. It is to the north. The Infinite, indeed, is all this."
Next follows the instruction about the Infinite with reference to "I": "I, indeed, am below. I am above. I am behind. I am before. I am to the south. I am to the north. I am indeed, all this."

✿   ✿   ✿

VII.25.2. Next follows the instruction about the Infinite with reference to the Self: "The Self, indeed, is below. It is above. It is behind. It is before. It is to the south. It is to the north. The Self, indeed, is all this. "
"Verily, he who sees this, reflects on this, and understands this delights in the Self, sports with the Self, rejoices in the Self, revels in the Self. Even while living in the body he becomes a self-ruler. He wields unlimited freedom in all the worlds."
"But those who think differently from this have others for their rulers; they live in perishable worlds. They have no freedom in all the worlds."

✿   ✿   ✿

VII.26.1. "For him who sees this, reflects on this, and understands this, the *prana* springs from the Self, hope springs from the Self, memory springs from the Self, the *akasha* springs from the Self, fire springs from the Self, water springs from the Self, appearance and disappearance spring from the Self, food springs from the Self, strength springs from the Self, understanding springs from the Self, meditation springs from the Self, consideration springs from the Self, will springs from the Self, mind springs from the Self, speech springs from the Self, the name springs from the Self, the sacred hymns spring from the Self, the sacrifices spring from the Self – ay, all this springs from the Self."

❂   ❂   ❂

Mundaka Upanishad

I.1.3. Saunaka, the great householder, approached Angiras in the proper manner and said: "Revered sir, what is that by the knowing of which all this becomes known?"

❂   ❂   ❂

I.1.4. To him he said: "Two kinds of knowledge must be known – that is what the knowers of *Brahman* tell us. They are the Higher Knowledge and the lower knowledge."

❂   ❂   ❂

I.1.5. "Of these two, the lower knowledge is the *Rig-Veda*, the *Yajur-Veda*, the *Sama-Veda*, the *Atharva-Veda*, *siksha* (phonetics), *kalpa* (rituals), *vyakaranam* (grammar), *nirukta* (etymology), *chhandas* (metre), and *jyotis* (astronomy); and the Higher Knowledge is that by which the Imperishable *Brahman* is attained."

🕉

I.1.6. "By means of the Higher Knowledge the wise behold everywhere *Brahman*, which otherwise cannot be seen or seized, which has no root or attributes, no eyes or ears, no hands or feet; which is eternal and omnipresent, all-pervading and extremely subtle; which is imperishable and the source of all beings."

❀ ❀ ❀

I.2.12. "Let a Brahmin, after having examined all these worlds that are gained by works, acquire freedom from desires: nothing that is eternal can be produced by what is not eternal."

❀ ❀ ❀

II.2.11. "That immortal *Brahman* alone is before, that *Brahman* is behind, that *Brahman* is to the right and left. *Brahman* alone pervades everything above and below; this universe is that Supreme *Brahman* alone."

❀ ❀ ❀

III.1.8. "Neither grasped by sight nor the other senses, nor by speech, nor penance, nor sacrifices; but made pure by brightness of understanding, then may one perceive It in meditation."

❀ ❀ ❀

III.2.5. "Having realized *Atman*, the seers become satisfied with that Knowledge. Their souls are established in the Supreme Self, they are free from passions, and they are tranquil in mind. Such calm souls ever devoted to the Self, behold everywhere the omnipresent *Brahman* and in the end enter into It, which is all this."

❀ ❀ ❀

III.2.8. "As flowing rivers disappear in the sea, losing their names and forms, so a wise man, freed from name and form, attains the *Purusha*, who is greater than the Great."

ॐ

III.2.9. "He who knows the Supreme *Brahman* verily becomes *Brahman*. In his family, no one is born ignorant of *Brahman*. He overcomes grief; he overcomes evil; free from the fetters of the heart, he becomes immortal."

❖   ❖   ❖

Taittiriya Upanishad

II.1.3. *OM*. He who knows *Brahman* attains the Supreme.
On the above, the following mantra is recorded:
"He who knows *Brahman* which is Reality, Knowledge and Infinity, hidden in the cave of the heart and in the highest ether (*akasha*) – he, being one with the omniscient *Brahman*, enjoys simultaneously all desires."
From the *Atman* was born ether; from ether, air; from air, fire; from fire, water; from water, earth; from earth, herbs; from herbs, food; from food, man.

❖   ❖   ❖

II.6.1. "If a person knows *Brahman* as non-existent, he himself becomes non-existent. If he knows *Brahman* as existent, then know him as existent."
...He desired: "May I be many, may I be born." He performed austerities. Having performed austerities, He created all this – whatever there is. Having created all this, He entered into it. Having entered into it, He became both the manifested and the unmanifested, both the defined and undefined, both the supported and unsupported, both the intelligent and the non-intelligent, both the real and the unreal. The *Satya* (the True) became all this; whatever there is. Therefore call It "the True".

🕉

II.7.1. "In the beginning all this was non-existent. From it was born what exists. That created Itself by Itself; therefore It is called the 'Self-made'."

...When a man finds fearless support in That which is invisible, incorporeal, indefinable and supportless, he has then obtained fearlessness.

If he makes the slightest differentiation in It, there is fear for him. That becomes fear for the knower who does not reflect.

❀ ❀ ❀

Kena Upanishad

I.3-4. The eye does not go thither, nor the speech, nor the mind. We do not know It; we do not understand how anyone can teach It. It is different from the known; It is above the unknown. Thus we have heard from the preceptors of old who taught It to us.

❀ ❀ ❀

I.5. That which cannot be expressed by speech, but by which speech is expressed – That alone know as *Brahman*, and not that which people here worship.

❀ ❀ ❀

I.6. That which cannot be apprehended by the mind, but by which, they say, the mind is apprehended – That alone know as *Brahman*, and not that which people here worship.

❀ ❀ ❀

I.7. That which cannot be perceived by the eye, but by which the eye is perceived – That alone know as *Brahman*, and not that which people here worship.

I.8. That which cannot he heard by the ear, but by which the hearing is perceived – That alone know as *Brahman*, and not that which people here worship.

❀ ❀ ❀

I.9. That which cannot be smelt by the breath, but by which the breath smells an object – That alone know as *Brahman*, and not that which people here worship.

❀ ❀ ❀

II.3. He by whom *Brahman* is not known, knows It; he by whom It is known, knows It not. It is not known by those who know It; It is known by those who do not know It.

❀ ❀ ❀

II.5. If a man knows *Atman* here, he then attains the true goal of life. If he does not know It here, a great destruction awaits him. Having realized the Self in every being, the wise relinquish the world and become immortal.

❀ ❀ ❀

Katha Upanishad

I.2.5. Fools dwelling in darkness, but thinking themselves wise and erudite, go round and round, by various tortuous paths, like the blind led by the blind.

❀ ❀ ❀

I.2.7. Many there are who do not even hear of *Atman*; though hearing of Him, many do not comprehend. Wonderful is the expounder and rare the hearer; rare indeed is the experiencer of *Atman* taught by an able preceptor.

1.2.12. The wise man who, by means of concentration on the Self, realizes that ancient, effulgent One, who is hard to be seen, unmanifested, hidden and who dwells in the *buddhi* and rests in the body – he, indeed, leaves joy and sorrow far behind.

❖   ❖   ❖

1.2.18. Spirit is not born, nor deceases ever, has not come from any, nor from it any. This Unborn, Eternal and Everlasting Ancient is not slain, be it slain the body.

❖   ❖   ❖

1.2.23. This *Atman* cannot be attained by the study of the *Veda*-s, or by intelligence, or by much hearing of sacred books. It is attained by him alone whom It chooses. To such a one *Atman* reveals Its own form.

❖   ❖   ❖

1.3.13. The wise man should merge his speech in his mind and his mind in his intellect. He should merge his intellect in the Cosmic Mind and the Cosmic Mind in the Tranquil Self.

❖   ❖   ❖

1.3.14. Arise! Awake! Approach the great and learn. Like the sharp edge of a razor is that path, so the wise say: "hard to tread and difficult to cross."

❖   ❖   ❖

II.1.11. By the mind alone is *Brahman* to be realized; then one does not see in It any multiplicity whatsoever. He goes from death to death who sees multiplicity in It. This, verily, is That.

❖   ❖   ❖

II.1.15. As pure water poured into pure water becomes one with it, so also, O Gautama, does the Self of the sage who knows.

ॐ

Isavashya Upanishad

5. It moves and moves not; It is far and likewise near. It is inside all this and It is outside all this.

❁   ❁   ❁

6. The wise man beholds all beings in the Self, and the Self in all beings; for that reason he does not hate anyone.

❁   ❁   ❁

7. To the seer, all things have verily become the Self: what delusion, what sorrow, can there be for him who beholds that oneness?

❁   ❁   ❁

10. One thing, they say, is obtained from knowledge; another, they say, from ignorance. Thus we have heard from the wise who have taught us this.

❁   ❁   ❁

Aitareya Upanishad

I.1.1. In the beginning (all) this verily was *Atman* only, one and without a second. There was nothing else that winked. He bethought Himself: "Let Me now create the worlds."

III.1.3. He is *Brahman*, He is Indra, He is *Prajapati*; He is all these gods; He is the five great elements – earth, air, *akasha* (space), water, light; He is all these small creatures and the others which are mixed (with them); He is the origin (of the moving and the unmoving) – those born of an egg, of a womb, of sweat, and of a sprout; He is horses, cows, human beings, elephants – whatever breathes here, whether moving on legs or flying in the air or unmoving. All this is guided by Consciousness (*Prajnanam*), is supported by Consciousness. The basis (of the universe) is Consciousness. Consciousness is *Brahman*.

Brahma Sutra

I.1.1. Hence, (is to be undertaken) thereafter a deliberation on *Brahman*.

❀   ❀   ❀

I.1.2. That (is *Brahman*) from which (are derived) the birth etc., of this (universe).

❀   ❀   ❀

I.1.3. (*Brahman* is omniscient) because of (Its) being the source of the scriptures.

❀   ❀   ❀

I.1.4. But that *Brahman* (is known from the *Upanishad*-s), (It) being the object of their fullest import.

❀   ❀   ❀

I.1.16. The other is not the Supreme Self, because that is illogical.

❀   ❀   ❀

I.1.19. Moreover, the scriptures teach the absolute identity of this one with this (One).

I.1.22. Space (*akasha*) is *Brahman*, for *Brahman*'s indicatory mark is in evidence.

✿ ✿ ✿

I.4.15. (Non-existence does not mean void), because of its allusion (to *Brahman*).

✿ ✿ ✿

II.1.15. (Cause and effect are non-different) since the effect is perceived when the cause is there.

✿ ✿ ✿

II.1.19. And the effect is non-different from the cause on the analogy of a piece of cloth.

✿ ✿ ✿

II.2.25. And (a permanent soul has to be admitted) because of the fact of remembrance (i.e. memory).

✿ ✿ ✿

II.2.26. Something does not come out of nothing, for this does not accord with experience.

✿ ✿ ✿

II.2.42. (The Bhagavata view that Samkarsana and others originate successively from Vasudeva and others is wrong), since any origin (for the soul) is impossible.

✿ ✿ ✿

II.3.3. (The Upanishadic passage about creation of space has) a secondary sense, for real creation is impossible.

II.3.6. The (Vedic) assertion (that "all things become known when the one is known") can remain unaffected only if all the effects are non-different from *Brahman*; and this is confirmed by Vedic texts.

❖ ❖ ❖

II.3.9. But (origin) for Existence (*Brahman*) is impossible on account of illogicality.

❖ ❖ ❖

II.3.17. The individual soul has no origin; because the *Upanishad*-s do not mention this, because its eternality is known from them, and because of other reasons.

❖ ❖ ❖

II.3.18. The soul is eternally a cognizer for this very reason (of being free from origin and dissolution).

❖ ❖ ❖

III.2.14. *Brahman* is only formless to be sure, for that is the dominant note (of the Upanishadic teaching).

❖ ❖ ❖

III.2.15. And like light, *Brahman* can (be assumed to) have different appearances, so that the scriptures may not become purportless.

❖ ❖ ❖

III.4.11. Knowledge and action are to be divided like a hundred things.

❖ ❖ ❖

III.4.16. Moreover, (from knowledge comes) the destruction (of the whole world).

IV.1.5. The sun, etc., are to be looked upon as *Brahman* because of the consequent exaltation.

❀ ❀ ❀

IV.2.16. (Absolute) non-distinction (with *Brahman* comes about) on the authority of the scriptural declaration.

❀ ❀ ❀

IV.4.1. Having reached the "Highest Light", the soul becomes manifest in its own real nature because of the use of the term "in its own" (in the *Upanishad*).

❀ ❀ ❀

IV.4.2. The soul then attains liberation, that being the (Upanishadic) declaration.

❀ ❀ ❀

IV.4.4. In liberation the soul exists in a state of inseparableness from the Supreme Self, for so it is noticed in the *Upanishad*.

❀ ❀ ❀

IV.4.6. Audulomi says that the liberated soul becomes established in consciousness itself, that being its true nature.

❀ ❀ ❀

IV.4.22. There is no return for the released souls on the strength of the Upanishadic declaration; there is no return for the related souls on the strength of the Upanishadic declaration.

Bhagavad Gita

II.16. Of the unreal no being there is; there is no non-being of the real. Of both these is the truth seen by the seers of the Essence.

❁   ❁   ❁

II.46. What utility there is in a reservoir by the side of an all-spreading flood of water, the same (utility) there is in all *Veda*-s for an enlightened *Brahmana*.

❁   ❁   ❁

III.3. In this world a twofold path was taught by Me at first, O sinless one; that of *Sankhya*-s by devotion of knowledge, and that of *Yogin*-s by devotion to action.

❁   ❁   ❁

IV.24. *Brahman* is the offering, *Brahman* the oblation; by *Brahman* is the oblation poured into the fire of *Brahman*; *Brahman* verily shall be reached by him who always sees *Brahman* in action.

❁   ❁   ❁

V.8-9. "I do nothing at all"; thus would the truth-knower think, steadfast – though seeing, hearing, touching, smelling, eating, going, sleeping, breathing, speaking, letting go, seizing, opening and closing the eyes – remembering that the senses move among sense-objects.

✿ ✿ ✿

VI.9. He is esteemed, who is of the same mind in the good-hearted, friends, foes, the indifferent, the neutral, the hateful, relatives, the righteous, and the unrighteous.

✿ ✿ ✿

VI.25. Little by little let him withdraw, by reason (*buddhi*) held in firmness; keeping the mind established in the Self, let him not think of anything.

✿ ✿ ✿

VII.24. The foolish regard Me as the unmanifested coming in manifestation, knowing not My higher, immutable, unsurpassed nature.

✿ ✿ ✿

IX.24. I am indeed the Enjoyer, as also the Lord, of all sacrifices; but they do not know Me in truth; whence they fail.

✿ ✿ ✿

IX.34. Fix thy mind on Me, be devoted to Me, sacrifice to Me, bow down to Me. Thus steadied with Me as thy Supreme Goal, thou shalt reach Myself, the Self.

✿ ✿ ✿

X.4-5. Intelligence, wisdom, non-illusion, patience, truth, self-restraint, calmness, pleasure, pain, birth, death, fear, and security; innocence, equanimity, contentment, austerity, beneficence, fame, shame – (these) different kinds of dispositions of beings arise from Me alone.

ॐ

XII.5. Greater is their trouble whose thoughts are set on the Unmanifest; for, the Goal, the Unmanifest, is very hard for the embodied to reach.

❈   ❈   ❈

XIII.27. He sees who sees the Supreme Lord, remaining the same in all beings, the undying in the dying.

❈   ❈   ❈

XIII.29. He sees, who sees all actions performed by *Prakriti* alone and the Self not acting.

❈   ❈   ❈

XIV.17. From *Sattva* arises wisdom, and greed from *Rajas*; heedlessness and error arise from *Tamas*, and also ignorance.

❈   ❈   ❈

XIV.20. Having crossed beyond these three *guna*-s, which are the source of the body, the embodied one is freed from birth, death, decay and pain, and attains the immortal.

❈   ❈   ❈

XVIII.65. Fix thy thought on Me, be devoted to Me, worship Me, do homage to Me. Thou shalt reach Myself. The truth do I declare to thee; (for) thou art dear to Me.

ॐ

Yoga Vasishtha

I.18.34. The house that is the body which is the abode of all diseases, a place for wrinkles and old age and troublesome with the malady of all mental agonies, is not agreeable to me.

❀ ❀ ❀

I.19.2. Shame upon those, mad with the spirituous liquor of delusion, who have fixed their hope on their bodies and their stay in the world!

❀ ❀ ❀

I.21.1. What possibly is the beauty of a woman who is a puppet doll of flesh endowed with muscles, bones and joints in the string-tossed bodily cage?

❀ ❀ ❀

I.21.2. See if it is pleasing after separating the skin, flesh, blood, tears, eyes, etc. Why are you deluded in vain?

❀ ❀ ❀

I.21.10. Having limbs beautiful as the filaments of a flower, intent on destroying men, a lovely woman gives the insensibility of madness like a poisonous creeper.

I.21.12. Even at a great distance, women are indeed the agreeable and intense fuel for the burning fires of hell. They are insipid, though charming.

✿ ✿ ✿

I.26.9. Life is extremely transient, death is absolutely cruel, youth is very fickle and childhood is taken away by ignorance.

✿ ✿ ✿

I.31.12. In what ways the intense diseases of desire and hatred, multitudes of enjoyments and riches do not trouble a man wandering in the sea of worldly existence?

✿ ✿ ✿

III.1.12. The names of that Supreme Reality such as the Divine Law, the Self, the Supreme *Brahman* and the Truth are coined by learned men for the purpose of usage.

✿ ✿ ✿

III.5.5. Names such as "Self" are invented for the Absolute, from which words turn away (without defining it) and which is known by the liberated. They are not born from the inherent nature.

✿ ✿ ✿

III.5.6-7. He, who is the Soul (or the *Purusha*) for those having the view of the *Sankhya* philosophers, *Brahman* for the teachers of Vedanta, mere *Vijnana* (or intelligence), which is absolute and stainless, for the knowers of *Vijnana*, the Void for the expounders of the Void, and who is the illuminator of the rays of light of the sun, is always the Speaker, the Thinker, the Divine Law, the Enjoyer, the Seer and the Doer.

✿ ✿ ✿

III.6.1-2. In this matter (of attaining liberation), Knowledge is the practice; nothing else is employed. The highest fulfillment arises only from Knowledge; but not through the pain of religious practices.

❀ ❀ ❀

III.7.20. That is the nature of the Supreme Self in which great ocean of consciousness, there is only complete absence of the world as it stands.

❀ ❀ ❀

III.7.22. That is the nature of the Supreme Self, which is empty when there is a multitude of worlds, which void is, as it were, non-void, and in which the non-existent world exists.

❀ ❀ ❀

III.7.31. The highest (or Absolute) Reality is not known at any time by anybody without (realizing) the impossibility of the natural existence of this visible object, called the world.

❀ ❀ ❀

III.9.14. Having given up the position of one liberated while living, when the body is overcome by time (or death), he enters the state of one liberated without a body, as wind (attains to) motionlessness.

❀ ❀ ❀

III.9.23. Whatever of this (world) appears, appeared, or will attain to appearance, He is quite every visible object existing in the three times, past, present and future.

❀ ❀ ❀

III.9.25. Rama! This is called liberation. This is declared as *Brahman* (or the Absolute Reality). This is described as Nirvana (or extinction of individuality and absorption in the Supreme Spirit), having a form which is fuller than the full.

ॐ

III.10.17. The Light of the Absolute, who is of the nature of the sky, is only Self-experience. That One who is within, is experienced only by Himself; not by another.

❀ ❀ ❀

III.11.5. (This world) was neither born nor is subject to destruction. That which does not indeed exist in the beginning, of what sort could be its birth? What need now say of the word "destruction"?

❀ ❀ ❀

III.13.40. Nothing whatever is accomplished, nothing is born and nothing is perceived. There is neither falsity nor reality. This is some indescribable unborn entity which is spread.

❀ ❀ ❀

III.13.48-49. Even when the perception of the world is born, nothing whatever is born. The Supreme Sky (of Consciousness), void all around and clear, is alone settled.

❀ ❀ ❀

III.21.58. There could be the course of destruction or the opposite only in that which verily exists. Of what sort could be the destruction of that which does not at all exist in fact?

❀ ❀ ❀

III.21.72. Therefore, there is neither absence of discrimination, nor nescience, nor bondage, nor liberation. This world is Pure Consciousness which is undisturbed.

❀ ❀ ❀

III.22.24. Wise men consider thinking of That, describing That, instructing one another about That and sole devotion to This alone, as Practice.

III.22.28. "This visible world was not born even at the beginning of creation. Therefore, this world and I (or the ego) just do not exist at all times." Thus, the practice of knowledge is declared.

❖ ❖ ❖

III.22.31. The perception of the absence of the visible world is indeed declared as knowledge as well as the Reality to be known. Final liberation (arises) by its practice. Thus, the practice is great elevation.

❖ ❖ ❖

III.40.44. Thus, this delusion of the world has grown quite falsely. It is like the union with a dream-woman. Though experienced, it consists of unreality.

❖ ❖ ❖

III.40.57. The Universe does not exist without thinking.

❖ ❖ ❖

III.42.4. As the unreal dream-death of a living being, appearing like reality, shines causing an action that can be perceived by the senses (such as weeping, expression of sorrow, etc.,), so, the world exists for those with foolish (or perplexed) intellects.

❖ ❖ ❖

III.42.18. If these cities and inhabitants are not real in a dream, then, they are not real for me even a little, here (in the waking state) also, which is of the same form (or nature).

❖ ❖ ❖

III.42.20. As I am a reality for you in the worldly existence which is a large dream, so, you are also a reality for me. Everything (happens) in dreams. So is the manner (of cognition).

🕉

III.52.42. Since *Brahman* (or the Ultimate Reality) is existing everywhere, when, where and in which manner anything is born, there and in that manner, one perceives it immediately, only by the power (akin to) a dream.

❀ ❀ ❀

III.54.21. This is only unreality resembling reality and is an appearance. It is uncreated, yet experienced. It is not real, but exists as reality.

❀ ❀ ❀

III.54.67. The conscious person or the soul neither dies nor is born anywhere. It only perceives this mistakenly like the confusion (arising) in a dream.

❀ ❀ ❀

III.54.69. Say, who (has seen) consciousness dead till this day – whose, which and how? Hundreds of thousands of bodies die. Consciousness is remaining imperishable.

❀ ❀ ❀

III.57.50. As dreaming is, so is this waking. There is no doubt in this matter. An unreal city appears in a dream. At the beginning of creation, the unreal world appears.

❀ ❀ ❀

III.61.24. As a doll, not yet carved, exists (potentially) in the clay and in the block of wood (used for making the doll) and as letters exist (potentially) in a paste of ink, so, the world exists in the Supreme Spirit.

❀ ❀ ❀

III.65.12. As there is no duality (or difference) between the Conscious Self (or *Brahman*) and the individual soul, so also,

🕉

there is no difference between the individual soul and the mind. As there is no difference between the individual soul and the mind, so also, there is no difference between the body and (its) actions.

❀ ❀ ❀

III.66.8. As a drunken person sees trees as whirling on account of intoxication, so, the individualized consciousness perceives the worlds which are excited by the mind.

❀ ❀ ❀

III.67.68. There is the destruction of the perceptions from *Brahma* (the Creator-god) to a worm, on account of right knowledge.

❀ ❀ ❀

III.67.76. This (world) has arisen falsely; it grows falsely; it pleases falsely; and it perishes falsely.

❀ ❀ ❀

III.67.79. The Self is spontaneously perceived, as if it were another, only by itself.

❀ ❀ ❀

III.95.3. Rama! Where the conduct of unenlightened persons is observed, there, statements of the nature, "individual souls are born from *Brahman*", exist.

❀ ❀ ❀

III.96.25. The essential nature of the Self is pure (or stainless). A second view which is stained is brought into existence only without being understood. Then, it is declared as ignorance (*avidya*).

ॐ

III.96.29. It reduces reality to unreality immediately or pure being to a living being instantly. This is an error relating to reality and unreality. Because of that, it is described as illusion (*maya*).

❀   ❀   ❀

III.100.42. The delusion of bondage, liberation and the like does not exist even a little for a wise person. Rama! Delusion, bondage, liberation and the like exist only for the ignorant.

❀   ❀   ❀

III.114.23. The mind is bound on account of firm idea, "I am not *Brahman*".

❀   ❀   ❀

III.119.25. In the Absolute Peace, the Supreme Spirit indeed exists in this manner through "this-ness". There is no creation here. There is nothing whatever by name "creation" at any time.

❀   ❀   ❀

IV.1.21. This objective world exists (in *Brahman*) as a sprout within a seed at the time of the great sleep (or dissolution of the world). Whoever declares thus, it is only ignorance. He has (the ignorance of) childhood.

❀   ❀   ❀

IV.2.8. Rama! Therefore, the world was not, is not, and will not be (in the Absolute). It is only the Space of Consciousness that shines, as it were, in its own Self, directly in this manner.

❀   ❀   ❀

IV.38.7. What the mind does, that is done; what it does not do, that is not done. Therefore, the mind alone is the doer; not the body.

ॐ

IV.39.21. This (doctrine that everything is *Brahman*) when displayed (or revealed), surely does not befit one whose intellect is half-learned. Contemplating with the perception of enjoyment that brings objects (before the mind), this person perishes.

❀ ❀ ❀

IV.39.24. Whoever tells an ignorant person, who is half-awakened, that everything is *Brahman*, that ignorant person is joined (or dispatched) to a multitude of big hells by him.

❀ ❀ ❀

IV.40.17. Rama! This formation of words such as, "(the world) is brought into existence by That (Absolute) or it has arisen from That (Absolute)," is for usage in scriptures; not really (or from the Absolute point of view).

❀ ❀ ❀

IV.40.34. From that infinite abode of *Brahman* which is the All and all-pervading, nothing different whatever arises. Therefore, what arises, that is only That (*Brahman*).

❀ ❀ ❀

IV.45.45. What does not exist at the beginning and the end, is so at the present also. Of what nature could the reality be, of a thing that does not exist at the beginning and the end?

❀ ❀ ❀

IV.57.26. Let him perform or not perform works as also absorption in the Supreme Spirit (or *samadhi*). The one who has given up all efforts (or hopes) by the mind has (reached) the highest abode and is already liberated.

ॐ

V.5.1. That which is constant at the beginning and the end is called Real; not the rest. What is real at the beginning and the end, is only real when existing (at the present).

❖   ❖   ❖

V.5.25. Human Beings! There is not even a little relationship of this stainless Self with the body, as (there is no relationship) of gold with a particle of mud, though situated in it.

❖   ❖   ❖

V.18.62. "There is no place where I am not; there is nothing which is not mine." Having ascertained in this manner, the intellect of the wise (or self-possessed ones) is quite free from coverings (or restraints).

❖   ❖   ❖

V.29.10. For what reason (or from what) do I desire liberation? By whom indeed am I bound hitherto? I desire liberation, not being bound. What is this childish mockery?

❖   ❖   ❖

V.29.11. There is neither bondage nor liberation. My stupidity has come to an end. What is the use of my playing with meditation and what would happen to me by not meditating?

❖   ❖   ❖

V.29.15. I am not dead, nor do I live. I am neither being nor non-being nor made of anything real. This (objective world) is not mine; nor also is a different one mine. Salutations to me! I am extensive (or infinite).

❖   ❖   ❖

V.43.16. If a spiritual preceptor raises an ignorant person without his own effort, then, for what reason does he not raise (or liberate) a camel, or a tamed bull?

ॐ

V.43.17. Whatever that is great is got for one's self from one's own mind which has been conquered, that is not obtained even a little from God *Hari*, from the *Guru* (or spiritual preceptor) or from wealth.

❀ ❀ ❀

V.54.72. Embodied beings, having reached through their heart (or intellect) that position of Supreme Bliss, do not value the visible world, as kings (do not value) poverty.

❀ ❀ ❀

V.74.44. Desirelessness is the greatest happiness – greater than even sovereignty, the heaven, the moon, the spring season, or union with a lovely woman.

❀ ❀ ❀

V.77.25. He takes or leaves everything in everyway and behaves like a child without anything to be chosen.

❀ ❀ ❀

V.79.3. Right perception is the conviction that these hundreds of groups of objects having forms like jars, garments, etc., are only the Self and nothing else exists.

❀ ❀ ❀

V.89.17. Here, one who is self-possessed, who has gone beyond everything, who is free from seekings and is satisfied only in the Self, neither acts nor desires.

❀ ❀ ❀

V.89.18. For him, there is no purpose (served) by moving in the sky, by enjoyments, by dignity, by honors, or by hopes, life and death.

ॐ

VI/1.2.28. That Supreme *Brahman*, of the nature of Consciousness, is perceived in the lower world, on the earth, in the heaven, in a blade of grass and also in the heart of a living creature. There is indeed nothing else.

❖ ❖ ❖

VI/1.6.6. The Self is not related to the body and there is no body in the Self. These are mutually different as light and darkness.

❖ ❖ ❖

VI/1.9.20. The perception of knowledge and ignorance do not exist. Be one whose feet are firmly rooted in the residual Reality. There is nothing like ignorance or knowledge. Enough of this fancy.

❖ ❖ ❖

VI/1.11.16. Whatever of this extensive network of worlds is seen, all that is the stainless *Brahman*. This is settled.

❖ ❖ ❖

VI/1.11.90. I am that stainless one, who is the Consciousness (existing) always within and outside the multitude of objects such as a mountain, in the form of general Existence.

❖ ❖ ❖

VI/1.29.128. Know that as the worship of the Deity, in which the Self-God is worshipped by flowers in the form of tranquility and awareness. The worship of a form is not worship.

❖ ❖ ❖

VI/1.33.42. This falsity of the world has risen only as mere imagination. Sage! It vanishes somewhere by the mere absence of imagination.

VI/1.39.50. Let one worship the Self always, abandoning what is not desired as well as what is desired and also by accepting both.

❖ ❖ ❖

VI/1.42.16. Consciousness, in the form of imagination, causes all the show in consciousness. The world is like the creation, falling down and flying up of a dream-city.

❖ ❖ ❖

VI/1.48.12. It is neither existence nor non-existence nor intermediate. It is not also emptiness or the absence of it. It does not exist nor does it not exist. It is not quite within the scope of speech.

❖ ❖ ❖

VI/1.49.17. The manner of understanding such as, "this is *avidya* (or nescience); this is *jiva* (or the individual soul)", has been fashioned by the best among knowers of words for the instruction of the unenlightened.

❖ ❖ ❖

VI/1.49.23. I am *Brahman*. The triple world is *Brahman*. You are indeed *Brahman*. The visible universe (is also *Brahman*). There is no second perception. Do as you wish.

❖ ❖ ❖

VI/1.51.13. That alone is indeed the nature of Nescience consisting of unreality, on which account, while being observed, it certainly perishes and is not seen at all.

❖ ❖ ❖

VI/1.93.62. Everything is indeed given to him who does not take anything whatever. Quite everything waits upon him who gives up everything.

🕉

VI/1.95.3. How could *Brahman*, the Absolute Reality, which is not a doer, action or instrument, which is causeless, without a seed, and not fit to be discussed or understood, become a creator (of the world)?

❈   ❈   ❈

VI/1.95.17. On account of the absence of a cause, this world is not the work of anybody. Due to the absence of causality, there is also the absence of effect. Know this world as (appearing) on account of delusion.

❈   ❈   ❈

VI/1.96.17. That Supreme Reality is so great that, in front of it, this world appears like an atom and, sometimes, does not at all appear.

❈   ❈   ❈

VI/1.98.8. The words of the unintelligent that *Ishvara* (or the Supreme Lord), who is nameless, invincible, formless and his own Self, creates the world, are only to be laughed at.

❈   ❈   ❈

VI/1.99.8. Son! This space of Consciousness which shines clearly, that indeed appears as the world. There is no other world (different from Consciousness).

❈   ❈   ❈

VI/1.108.20. All creatures, of whatever nature, strive only for happiness.

❈   ❈   ❈

VI/1.111.31. The giving up of the ego (or the sense of "I" which is the root of all thoughts) is easier to perform than even the splitting off of a flower or the winking of the eyes. There is not even a little trouble in this matter.

ॐ

VI/1.115.36. He is called a great renouncer who has the conviction within in this manner: "There is no body for me, nor even birth, nor proper or improper actions."

❀ ❀ ❀

VI/1.125.1. The settled doctrine of scriptures expounding the nature of the Supreme Spirit is only the denial of everything (other than *Brahman*). There is no Nescience here, not Illusion. This (Universe) is the tranquil *Brahman* without a course.

❀ ❀ ❀

VI/2.1.3. The knowers (of the process) of imagination declare only the "I-thought" (or the feeling of "I") as imagination. Contemplation of that ("I-thought") in the sense of the space (of Consciousness) is called the renunciation of imagination.

❀ ❀ ❀

VI/2.8.3. That ego, being looked at, certainly does not exist at any time. (When investigated by inward contemplation, the ego vanishes). Its knowledge is only so much. By this (investigation) alone, it is destroyed completely.

❀ ❀ ❀

VI/2.9.27. What is the use of many words in this matter? This is declared briefly (as follows): "Imagination is the bondage of the mind. Its absence is the state of liberation."

❀ ❀ ❀

VI/2.25.12. The object which is known by consciousness is declared only as consciousness. Consciousness does not know the unconscious because of the difference in nature. Therefore there is no otherness.

❀ ❀ ❀

VI/2.37.33. When the visible object, reduced to the state of insipidity, does not please anywhere, then, desire does not arise. Then alone, there is the state of liberation.

❖ ❖ ❖

VI/2.52.7. Without expressing doubts such as, "Whence is this *avidya* and how (does it arise)?" you will understand yourself from Knowledge (or Enlightenment) that neither this (world) exists nor this (*avidya*).

❖ ❖ ❖

VI/2.60.28. The instrument of action, the action, the doer, birth, death and existence, everything is only *Brahman*. There is indeed no other idea without That.

❖ ❖ ❖

VI/2.62.27. That (Absolute Reality) is not expressible in words, un-manifest, beyond the (cognizance of the) senses and nameless. Its true nature is indeed not the subject-matter of the teaching of scholars.

❖ ❖ ❖

VI/2.93.73. All riches are calamities. Pleasure is only for (experiencing) pain. Life is only for (experiencing) death. Alas! What an illusory sport!

❖ ❖ ❖

VI/2.93.84. The splendors of youth are transient like the shadows of autumnal clouds. Objects of sense are pleasing at first sight, (but) causing pain at the end.

❖ ❖ ❖

VI/2.149.41. In that of the nature of All, everything exists everywhere, in every way and always. So, in the Supreme Reality, everything exists everywhere, always and of the nature of everything.

ॐ

VI/2.151.10. You are a person of our dream and we are persons of your dream. Thus, all this here (i.e. individuals and objects) are mutually existing like a dream (in each other's mind).

❋ ❋ ❋

VI/2.174.24. (Liberation is obtained) not by places of pilgrimage, nor by charity, nor by religious ablution, nor by learning, nor by meditation, nor by Yoga, nor by religious austerities, nor by sacrifices.

❋ ❋ ❋

VI/2.176.5. As the primary Absolute Consciousness alone shines in itself as world-nature in a dream, so also, at the beginning of creation, nothing other than (*Brahman*) is produced here.

❋ ❋ ❋

VI/2.195.38. "The world with a huge form exists in *Brahman* which is formless, as a gem within a casket." This can only be the word of a mad person.

❋ ❋ ❋

VI/2.195.44. Therefore, an unreal appearance like a dream, by way of manifoldness of form such as creation, is existing in the conscious Self. The Supreme Self is formless.

❋ ❋ ❋

VI/2.210.11. All that is here is mere thought.

❋ ❋ ❋

VI/2.213.11. Son! This (nescience) does not at all perish since it does not exist. There is no existence of the unreal. There is no non-existence of the real.

ॐ

Stories from Yoga Vasishtha

The story of the three unborn children

A mother once told the following story to amuse her child. In a city which never existed, there lived three princes, two of whom were never born and the third never entered the womb of any mother. They once went out and took their bath in three rivers, two of which were already dried up and the third never had any water at all. There they stayed in three houses, two of which never existed and the third was not yet built. Then they invited three guests, two of whom had no mouth and the third no stomach.

❖ ❖ ❖

The story of a Mithya-Purusha (Unreal Man)

There was a *mithya-purusha* (unreal man) who wanted to encase space. For this purpose he makes a jar, but after some time the jar is broken, living the man bewailing the loss of the space that was enclosed in the jar. Then he digs a well, constructs a tank, and builds a four-storeyed house. But all these things come to destruction, one after another. The man bewailing the futility of his efforts to preserve space in a finite form, dies at last.

❖ ❖ ❖

ॐ

The story of a Block of Stone

Once Vasishtha himself wanted to meditate in a solitary place. Finding disturbances everywhere, even in the ether-real plane, he retires to the *Shunya* plane. There he imagines a hut in which he sits in *samadhi*. In that state, he experiences and wanders through innumerable worlds, one within the other. Waking up from the *samadhi* state, he happens to hear a sweet and melodious song and through his *akasha-dharana* (meditation on the ether), he finds out the source of the enchanting song to be a beautiful woman, who, when requested, tells him that, in a corner of the world imagined by him, there is a mountain. Within a point on a stone of that mountain, she and her husband are living. They both stand in need of Self-knowledge for which she requests Vasishtha. The latter becomes curious, accompanies her, and finds her husband there. The *Brahmana*, her husband, having attained Self-knowledge sits in *Nirvikalpa-samadhi*, and thereby the world of his *sankalpa* (imagination) collapses. This fact is seen by Vasishtha through meditation. Returning therefrom, Vasishtha comes back to his own hut, but finds that his own body, which was left in his hut, is entered by the soul of a *siddha*. Vasishtha having withdrawn the force of his own *sankalpa* (imagination) which created the hut, the hut collapses along with the body within it, and the *siddha* consequently falls down to the earth. Vasishtha explains the matter to him, and both go to the *Siddhaloka* and live there.

❖   ❖   ❖

ॐ

The story of a Chintamani (philosopher's stone)

A man was in search of a philosopher's stone. He happened to find it accidentally. But he thought that philosopher's stone was a too valuable thing to be found so easily and that he was too unfortunate to find it so soon. He therefore threw it away, thinking it to be a piece of glass. Throwing it away, he proceeded further and reached a forest where, in spite of his repeated efforts, he finds nothing but pieces of glass.

Ashtavakra Gita

I.4. If only you will remain resting in consciousness, seeing yourself as distinct from the body, then even now you will become happy, peaceful and free from bonds.

❀ ❀ ❀

I.7. You are the one witness of everything, and are always completely free. The cause of your bondage is that you see the witness as something other than this.

❀ ❀ ❀

I.11. If one thinks of oneself as free, one is free, and if one thinks of oneself as bound, one is bound. Here this saying is true, "Thinking makes it so".

❀ ❀ ❀

I.15. You are really unbound and actionless, self-illuminating and spotless already. The cause of your bondage is that you are still resorting to stilling the mind.

❀ ❀ ❀

I.7. From ignorance of oneself, the world appears, and by knowledge of oneself, it appears no longer. From ignorance of the rope, it appears to be a snake, and by knowledge of it, it does so no longer.

II.17. I am pure awareness though through ignorance I have imagined myself to have additional attributes. By continually reflecting like this, my dwelling place is in the Unimagined.

✿   ✿   ✿

II.18. I have neither bondage nor freedom. Having lost its support the illusion has ceased. Oh, the universe, though existing in me, does not in reality so exist.

✿   ✿   ✿

II.20. The body, heaven and hell, bondage and liberation, and fear too, all this is pure imagination. What is there left to do for me whose very nature is consciousness?

✿   ✿   ✿

II.25. How wonderful it is that in the Infinite Ocean of myself, the waves of living beings arise, collide, play and disappear, in accordance with their nature.

✿   ✿   ✿

III.3. Having known yourself to be That in which the universe appears like waves on the sea, why do you run about like a miserable being?

✿   ✿   ✿

III.4. After hearing of oneself as pure consciousness and the supremely beautiful, is one to go on lusting after sordid sexual objects?

✿   ✿   ✿

III.5. When the sage has realized that he himself is in all beings, and all beings are in him, it is astonishing that the sense of individuality should be able to continue.

ॐ

III.12. With whom can we compare that great-souled one who is content with Self-knowledge and does not hanker even after liberation?

❀ ❀ ❀

Janaka said:

VI.1. Boundless like space am I and the phenomenal world is like a jar; this is knowledge. So it has neither to be renounced nor accepted nor destroyed.

❀ ❀ ❀

VI.2. I am like the ocean, and the universe is like the wave; this is knowledge. So it has neither to be renounced nor accepted nor destroyed.

❀ ❀ ❀

VI.3. I am like the mother of pearl and the illusion of the universe is like the silver; this is knowledge. So it has neither to be renounced nor accepted nor destroyed.

❀ ❀ ❀

VI.4. I am indeed in all beings, and all beings are in me. This is knowledge. So it has neither to be renounced nor accepted nor destroyed.

❀ ❀ ❀

VIII.1. Bondage is when the mind longs for something, grieves about something, rejects something, holds on to something, is pleased about something or displeased about something.

❀ ❀ ❀

VIII.2. Liberation is when the mind does not long for anything, grieve about anything, reject anything, or hold on to anything, and is not pleased about anything or displeased about anything.

ॐ

IX.3. All this is transient and spoilt by the three sorts of pain. Knowing it to be insubstantial, ignoble and fit only for rejection, one attains peace.

✿ ✿ ✿

X.1. Cultivate indifference to everything, having given up *kama* (desire) which is the enemy, *artha* (worldly prosperity) which is attended with mischief and *dharma* (performance of good works) which is the cause of these two.

✿ ✿ ✿

X.2. Look upon friends, lands, wealth, houses, wives, presents, and other such marks of good fortune as a dream or a juggler's show lasting only a few days.

✿ ✿ ✿

X.3. Know that wherever there is desire there is the world. Betaking yourself to firm non-attachment, go beyond desire, and be happy.

✿ ✿ ✿

X.4. Bondage consists only in desire, and the destruction of desire is said to be liberation. Only by non-attachment to the world does one attain the constant joy of the realization of the Self.

✿ ✿ ✿

X.5. You are one, conscious and pure, while all this is inert non-being. Ignorance itself is nothing, so what is the point of wanting to understand?

✿ ✿ ✿

X.6. Kingdoms, children, wives, bodies, pleasures – these have all been lost to you life after life, attached to them though you were.

🕉

X.7. Enough of wealth, sensuality and good deeds. In the forest of *samsara* the mind has never found satisfaction in these.

❀ ❀ ❀

X.8. How many births have you not done hard and painful labor with body, mind and speech? Now at last, stop!

❀ ❀ ❀

XI.6. Realizing "I am not the body, nor is the body mine. I am awareness", one attains the supreme state and no longer remembers things done or undone.

❀ ❀ ❀

XI.8. He who knows for certain that this manifold and wonderful universe is nothing, becomes desireless and Pure Consciousness, and finds peace as if nothing exists.

❀ ❀ ❀

XII.1. I became intolerant first of physical action, then of extensive speech, and then of thought. Thus verily do I therefore abide.

❀ ❀ ❀

XIII.3. Recognizing that in reality no action is ever committed, I live as I please, just doing what presents itself to be done.

❀ ❀ ❀

XIII.5. No benefit or loss comes to me by standing, walking or lying down, so consequently I live as I please whether standing, walking or sleeping.

❀ ❀ ❀

XIV.3. As I have realized the Supreme Self who is the Witness and the Lord, and have become indifferent to both bondage and liberation, I feel no anxiety for emancipation.

ॐ

XIV.4. The different conditions of one who within is devoid of doubts but outwardly moves about at his own pleasure like a deluded person, can only be understood by those like him.

❀ ❀ ❀

Ashtavakra said:
XV.1. While a man of pure intelligence may achieve the goal by the most casual of instruction, another may seek knowledge all his life and still remain bewildered.

❀ ❀ ❀

XV.3. This awareness of the truth makes an eloquent, clever and energetic man dumb, stupid and lazy, so it is avoided by those whose aim is enjoyment.

❀ ❀ ❀

XV.7. Your nature is the consciousness, in which the whole world wells up, like waves in the sea. That is what you are, without any doubt, so be free of disturbance.

❀ ❀ ❀

XV.8. Have faith, my son, have faith. Don't let yourself be deluded in this. You are yourself the Lord, whose very nature is knowledge, and you are beyond natural causation.

❀ ❀ ❀

XV.9. The body invested with the senses, stands still, and comes and goes. You yourself neither come nor go, so why bother about them?

❀ ❀ ❀

XV.10. Let the body last to the end of the Age, or let it come to an end right now. What have you gained or lost, who consist of pure consciousness?

XV.11. Let the world wave rise or subside according to its own nature in you, the great ocean. It is no gain or loss to you.

❖ ❖ ❖

XV.12. My son, you consist of pure consciousness, and the world is not separate from you. So who is to accept or reject it, and how, and why?

❖ ❖ ❖

XV.13. How can there be either birth, karma or responsibility in that one unchanging, peaceful, unblemished and infinite consciousness which is you?

❖ ❖ ❖

XV.18. Only one thing has existed, exists and will exist in the ocean of being. You have no bondage or liberation. Live happily and fulfilled.

❖ ❖ ❖

XV.19. Being pure consciousness, do not disturb your mind with thoughts of for and against. Be at peace and remain happy in yourself, the essence of joy.

❖ ❖ ❖

XV.20. Give up meditation completely but don't let the mind hold on to anything. You are free by nature, so what will you achieve by forcing the mind?

❖ ❖ ❖

Ashtavakra said:
XVI.1. My son, you may recite or listen to countless scriptures, but you will not be established within until you can forget everything.

🕉

XVI.4. Happiness belongs to no-one but that supremely lazy man for whom even opening and closing his eyes is a bother.

❊   ❊   ❊

XVI.11. If even Shiva, Vishnu or the lotus-born Brahma were your instructor, until you have forgotten everything you cannot be established within.

❊   ❊   ❊

XVII.5. Those who desire pleasure and those who desire liberation are both found in *samsara*, but the great-souled man who desires neither pleasure nor liberation is rare indeed.

❊   ❊   ❊

XVII.6. It is only the noble minded who is free from attraction or repulsion to religion, wealth, sensuality, and life and death too.

❊   ❊   ❊

XVII.8. Being fulfilled by the knowledge of the Self and with his mind absorbed, and contented, the wise one lives happily, seeing, hearing, touching, smelling and tasting.

❊   ❊   ❊

XVII.9. In him for whom the ocean of *samsara* has dried up, there is neither attachment nor aversion. His gaze is vacant, his behavior purposeless, and his senses inactive.

❊   ❊   ❊

XVII.13. The liberated man is free from desires everywhere. He neither blames, praises, rejoices, is disappointed, gives, nor takes.

XVII.14. When a great-souled one is unperturbed in mind, and equally self-possessed at either the sight of a woman inflamed with desire or at approaching death, he is truly liberated.

❀   ❀   ❀

XVIII.5. The Self which is absolute, effortless, immutable, and spotless is neither far away nor limited. It is verily ever-attained.

❀   ❀   ❀

XVIII.7. Knowing everything as just imagination, and himself as eternally free, how should the wise man behave like a fool?

❀   ❀   ❀

XVIII.14. There is no delusion, world, meditation on That, or liberation for the pacified great soul. All these things are just the realm of imagination.

❀   ❀   ❀

XVIII.28. He who is beyond mental stillness and distraction, does not desire either liberation or its opposite. Recognizing that things are just constructions of the imagination, that great soul lives as *Brahman* here and now.

❀   ❀   ❀

XVIII.34. The stupid does not attain cessation whether he acts or abandons action, while the wise man finds peace within simply by knowing the truth.

❀   ❀   ❀

XVIII.36. The stupid does not achieve liberation even through regular practice, but the fortunate remains free and actionless simply by understanding.

XVIII.37. The stupid does not attain *Brahman* because he wants
to become it, while the wise man enjoys the Supreme *Brahman*
without even wanting it.

❀   ❀   ❀

XVIII.56. Even when pleased he is not pleased, not suffering
even when in pain. Only those like him can know the
wonderful state of such a man.

❀   ❀   ❀

XVIII.57. It is the feeling that there is something that needs to
be achieved which is *samsara*. The wise who are of the form of
emptiness, formless, unchanging and spotless see nothing of
the sort.

❀   ❀   ❀

XVIII.58. Even when doing nothing the fool is agitated by
restlessness, while a skillful man remains undisturbed even
when doing what there is to do.

❀   ❀   ❀

XVIII.59. Happy he stands, happy he sits, happy he sleeps, and
happy he comes and goes. Happy he speaks, and happy he
eats. This is the life of a man at peace.

❀   ❀   ❀

XVIII.67. Glorious is he who is free from all desires, who is the
perfect embodiment of bliss which is his own nature, and who
is spontaneously absorbed in the unconditioned Self.

❀   ❀   ❀

XVIII.70. The pure man who has experienced the Indescribable
attains peace by virtue of his very nature, realizing that all this
is nothing but illusion, and that nothing is.

XVIII.76. A fool does not get rid of his stupidity even on hearing the truth. He may appear outwardly free from imaginations, but inside he is still hankering after the senses.

❖ ❖ ❖

XVIII.77. Though in the eyes of the world he is active, the man who has shed action through knowledge finds no means of doing or speaking anything.

❖ ❖ ❖

XVIII.80. There is neither heaven nor hell nor even liberation during life. In a nutshell, in the sight of the seer nothing exists at all.

❖ ❖ ❖

XVIII.85. The wise man, who lives on whatever happens to come to him, roaming wherever he pleases, and sleeping wherever the sun happens to set, is at peace everywhere.

❖ ❖ ❖

XVIII.87. The wise man has the joy of being complete in himself and without possessions, acting as he pleases, free from duality and rid of doubts, and without attachment to any creature.

❖ ❖ ❖

XVIII.96. Neither happy nor unhappy, neither detached nor attached, neither seeking liberation nor liberated, he is neither something nor nothing.

❖ ❖ ❖

XVIII.97. Not distracted in distraction, in mental stillness not poised, in stupidity not stupid, that blessed one is not even wise in his wisdom.

ॐ

XIX.1. Using the tweezers of the knowledge of the truth I have managed to extract the painful thorn of endless opinions from the recesses of my heart.

❂ ❂ ❂

XIX.2. For me, established in my own glory, there are no religious obligations, sensuality, possessions, philosophy, duality or even non-duality.

❂ ❂ ❂

XIX.5. For me, established in my own glory, there is no dreaming or deep sleep, no waking, nor fourth state beyond them, and certainly no fear.

❂ ❂ ❂

XIX.8. To talk about the three ends of life is needless, to talk about yoga is purposeless, and even to talk about wisdom is irrelevant for me who reposes in the Self.

❂ ❂ ❂

XX.2. For me, free from the sense of dualism, there are no scriptures, no self-knowledge, no mind free from an object, no satisfaction and no freedom from desire.

❂ ❂ ❂

XX.3. There is no knowledge or ignorance, no "me", "this" or "mine", no bondage, no liberation, and no property of self-nature.

❂ ❂ ❂

XX.6. There is no world, no seeker for liberation, no *yogi*, no seer, no-one bound and no-one liberated. I remain in my own non-dual nature.

XX.7. There is no emanation or return, no goal, means, seeker or achievement. I remain in my own non-dual nature.

XX.12. For me, who am forever unmovable and indivisible, established in myself, there is no activity or inactivity, no liberation and no bondage.

❀ ❀ ❀

XX.13. For me, who am blessed and without limitation, there is no initiation or scripture, no disciple or teacher, and no goal of human life.

❀ ❀ ❀

XX.14. There is no being or non-being, no unity or dualism. What more is there to say? Nothing arises out of me.

Mandukya Karika

I.12. Neither the Self, nor others, nor truth nor even untruth: *prajna* knows nothing. *Turiya* is always all-seeing.

❀　❀　❀

I.17. If the phenomenal world were real, it would undoubtedly vanish. All this duality is mere *maya*. Non-duality is the Supreme Reality.

❀　❀　❀

I.18. If the multiplicity were imagined, it would vanish. Such doctrine is merely for the purpose of instruction. When known, duality ceases to exist.

❀　❀　❀

I.22. The man of conviction who knows the equal and common quality in each of the three states, he, the wise one, is worthy of the adoration and worship of all beings.

❀　❀　❀

I.26. *Pranava* is, indeed, the lower *Brahman*, and it is traditionally regarded as the higher *Brahman*. *Pranava* is unique, without cause, without precedent, without inside, without outside, absolute, immutable.

II.6. What does not exist in the beginning and does not exist at the end certainly does not in the middle! But like illusions, they seem real.

✿ ✿ ✿

II.12. Self-luminous *Atman*, by the power of its own *maya* imagines itself in itself. He alone is aware of the objects. This is the conclusion of the Vedanta.

✿ ✿ ✿

II.14. Those things that exist mentally as long as the thought lasts and the things likewise that exist objectively – all these are only imaginations. There is no other reason for the distinction.

✿ ✿ ✿

II.17. As a rope not definitely ascertained in the dark is imagined to be things like a snake, a line of water, etc., so also is the Self imagined.

✿ ✿ ✿

II.18. As imagination disappears when the rope is well-ascertained and there is the non-duality "This is only a rope", so also when the Self is well-ascertained.

✿ ✿ ✿

II.19. The Self is imagined to be the life-force (*prana*) and all these innumerable entities. This is the illusion of that shining one (i.e. the Self) by which it itself is deluded.

✿ ✿ ✿

II.29. Whatever may be displayed, that is the thing one sees. One becomes identified with it and satisfied by it. Engrossed in it he becomes absorbed in it.

ॐ

II.30. This Self is regarded as different owing only to these non-different objects. Whoever knows this truly may imagine the Self to be anything at all without any hesitation.

✿ ✿ ✿

II.32. There is no dissolution, no birth, none in bondage and none aspiring for wisdom, no seeker of liberation and none liberated. This is the Absolute Truth.

✿ ✿ ✿

II.34. From the standpoint of the Self the world does not exist; nor does it exist as independent, neither differentiated nor non-differentiated. This is what the wise know.

✿ ✿ ✿

II.36. Knowing It in this way, fix your memory on Non-duality. Having attained to the Non-dual, behave in the world like a mindless thing.

✿ ✿ ✿

II.38. Having seen the Reality within and in the world outside, he should become one with the Reality, find his delight in Reality and never deviate from Reality.

✿ ✿ ✿

III.1. Religious duty (*dharma*) associated with devotion arises when *Brahman* is supposed to have manifested Himself. Before birth everything is unborn (*aja*). Therefore religious duty is traditionally regarded as pitiable.

✿ ✿ ✿

III.2. Hence I shall speak of that which is not pitiable, which is without origination (*ajati*), which has gone to sameness. Thus those things, which are apparently being born on all sides are not born at all.

ॐ

III.3. For the Self, like space, arises as individual selves (*jiva*-s) like the pot-spaces. The aggregates are like the jars etc. This is the illustration of birth (*jati*).

❁ ❁ ❁

III.4. Just as when the pots etc., are dissolved, the pot-spaces etc., are completely merged into space, so the individual selves (*jiva*-s) are merged here in the Self (*Atman*).

❁ ❁ ❁

III.13. The identity without distinction of the *jiva* and the *Atman* is praised, and diversity is condemned. For only thus is all that tenable.

❁ ❁ ❁

III.14. The separateness, which is declared of the *jiva* and the *Atman* before origination is figurative, referring to the future. Its primary sense is certainly not reasonable.

❁ ❁ ❁

III.15. The creation which has been expounded by means of the examples of earth, metal, sparks (of fire) etc. is only a means of introducing the subject. There is no difference whatsoever.

❁ ❁ ❁

III.19. Non-duality becomes different only through illusion, for the unborn (*aja*) does not become different in any other way. For if, it became differentiated in reality, it would go the way of death.

❁ ❁ ❁

III.24. The *shruti* teaches: "There is no diversity here, etc.", and also "*Indra* by means of illusion, etc.", being birthless, he indeed is born through illusion in various ways.

🕉

III.25. And by the denial of birth, becoming is denied. In the *shruti* passage "Who again would give birth to it?" the cause of birth is denied.

❂ ❂ ❂

III.26. The *shruti* passage "He is not this, not this" denies what is explained. Therefore because all things are ungraspable they are declared to be birthless (*aja*).

❂ ❂ ❂

III.27. For the birth of the existent (*sat*) is reasonable through illusion, not however in reality. Indeed, to him for whom birth is real, the born is born!

❂ ❂ ❂

III.28. The birth of the nonexistent is not reasonable through illusion or reality, either. The son of a barren woman is not born either through illusion or in reality.

❂ ❂ ❂

III.31. This duality in whatever form, both the moving and the unmoving, is mind-perceived. For when the mind ceases to be mind, the duality is not perceived at all.

❂ ❂ ❂

III.32. When, as a result of the realization of the truth of the Self, the mind does not imagine, it goes to the state of being non-mind; in the absence of anything to grasp, it is non-grasping.

❂ ❂ ❂

III.33. They assert the knowledge free from imagination, birthless, not different from what is known. *Brahman* is that which is known, birthless, and eternal. The birthless knows the birthless.

III.36. *Brahman* is unborn, without sleep, without dream, without name, without form, ever shining, omniscient. There is no practicing whatsoever.

❀ ❀ ❀

III.38. There is no apprehension or abandonment where thought does not exist. Then knowledge is established in the Self, is unborn, and goes to the state of sameness.

❀ ❀ ❀

III.43. Keeping constantly in mind that everything is suffering, one should withdraw from the enjoyment of desires. Keeping constantly in mind the birthless, one indeed does not even see that which is born.

❀ ❀ ❀

III.46. When the mind does not go under, and when again it is not distracted, then that, motionless and without appearances, becomes *Brahman*.

❀ ❀ ❀

III.47. They say it rests in itself, is calm, is Nirvanic, indescribable, the highest bliss, omniscient, and is birthless with the birthless that is known.

❀ ❀ ❀

III.48. No *jiva* whatsoever is born. There is no becoming for it. This is the highest truth where nothing whatever is born.

❀ ❀ ❀

IV.4. There is no birth whatever of the existent; the nonexistent also is not born. Those dualists thus disputing amongst themselves assuredly proclaim birthlesness (*ajati*).

ॐ

IV.10. All *dharma*-s are intrinsically free from old age and death. By thinking of birth and death, those wishing to establish birth and death fall.

❀   ❀   ❀

IV.22. No thing whatsoever is born, either from itself or from another. No thing whatsoever – existent, nonexistent, or both existent and nonexistent – is born.

❀   ❀   ❀

IV.23. From the very nature of things, the cause, since it is beginningless, is not born, and the effect is not born either. If something has no beginning, one should not say that it does.

❀   ❀   ❀

IV.26. The mind does not touch an object, nor does it touch the appearance of an object, either. Since the object is nonexistent, the appearance of the object is nonexistent also.

❀   ❀   ❀

IV.27. The mind never touches any object (or cause) in the three periods of time. Being objectless (causeless), how could error arise in it?

❀   ❀   ❀

IV.28. Therefore, neither the mind nor what is perceived by the mind is born. Those who see its birth truly see a footprint in the sky.

❀   ❀   ❀

IV.29. Since it is the unborn that is said to be born, birthlessness is its very nature (*prakriti*). There can be no change in nature in any way whatever.

🕉

IV.30. Moreover, *samsara* would not have an end, nor would it be beginningless. And liberation (*moksha*), having a beginning, would not be endless.

❁ ❁ ❁

IV.31. That which does not exist at the beginning and at the end is such in the present also. Though they are on a par with things that are unreal, they are seen as if they were not unreal.

❁ ❁ ❁

IV.38. Since origination (*utpada*) is not established, it is declared that everything is unborn. There is no origination whatsoever of the nonexistent from the existent.

❁ ❁ ❁

IV.43. Those who are afraid of the doctrine of non-birth and who go astray owing to perception are not affected by the evil of *jati* (i.e. the doctrine that things are born). The evil will be of no great account.

❁ ❁ ❁

IV.45. Consciousness (*vijnana*), which has the appearance of birth, of motion, and of being a thing, is in reality unborn, unmoving, quiescent, non-dual (*advaya*), and lacks the character of being a thing.

❁ ❁ ❁

IV.46. Thus the mind is not born; thus *dharma*-s (entities) are traditionally taught to be unborn. Those alone who know this do not fall into error.

❁ ❁ ❁

IV.54. The *dharma-s* are not mind-born, and neither is the mind *dharma*-born. Thus the wise enter the birthlessness of cause and effect.

IV.55. As long as there is the preoccupation with cause and effect, so long is there the arising (*udbhava*) of cause and effect. When the preoccupation with cause and effect is destroyed, there is no arising of cause and effect.

❁ ❁ ❁

IV.56. As long as there is the preoccupation with cause and effect, so long does *samsara* continue. When the preoccupation with cause and effect is destroyed, *samsara* is no longer possible.

❁ ❁ ❁

IV.57. According to the relative truth (*samvriti*) everything is born; hence nothing is eternal (*sasvata*). In reality, however, everything is unborn; hence nothing is annihilated (*uccheda*).

❁ ❁ ❁

IV.58. Those *dharma*-s which are said to be born are in reality not born. Their birth is like an illusion, and that illusion itself does not exist.

❁ ❁ ❁

IV.71. No living being whatsoever is born; there is no becoming for it. This is that highest truth where nothing whatsoever is born.

❁ ❁ ❁

IV.73. What exists according to the imagined relative truth does not exist according to the absolute truth. What would exist according to the dependent relative truth does not exist in the absolute truth.

❁ ❁ ❁

IV.74. That which is unborn according to the imagined relative truth (*kalpita-samvriti*) is, according to the absolute truth, not even unborn. But it is born according to the relative truth which is a "dependent appearance" (*paratantrabhinispatti*).

❁ ❁ ❁

IV.75. There is persistent preoccupation with the nonexistent; but duality does not really exist. Only by realizing the nonexistence of duality one realizes its birthless, being free from causation.

❁ ❁ ❁

IV.79. When the mind is pre-occupied with the nonexistent, it turns toward that which is similar. Only by realizing the nonexistence of a thing, it turns away, unrelated to anything.

❁ ❁ ❁

IV.82. That Lord (*Bhagavan*) is always covered easily and uncovered with difficulty by the grasping of some *dharma* or other.

❁ ❁ ❁

IV.83. "Is", "is not", "is and is not" or again "neither is nor is not": the immature person thus covers the Lord over with notions of the moving, the steady, both, and the nonexistence of both.

❁ ❁ ❁

IV.84. These are the four alternatives (*kotya chatasra*) by the grasping of which the Lord is ever covered over. The Lord is untouched by these. He who sees this is all-seeing.

❁ ❁ ❁

IV.93. By their very nature (*prakriti*), all dharma-s are quiescent from the very beginning, unoriginated (*anutpanna*), completely unmodified, the same and non-different. The ultimate reality is birthless, uniform and free from fear (*visharada*).

IV.94. For those who are fascinated by multiplicity, wandering the pathways of duality, ever discoursing about plurality, there is no perfection. They are said to be pitiable.

❀ ❀ ❀

IV.95. Only those who are firm in their conviction with regard to the birthlessness and the uniformity become great knowers in this world. But the ordinary people of the world cannot understand this.

❀ ❀ ❀

IV.96. It is held that the birthless knowledge (*jnana*) does not pass over to the birthless *dharma*-s. Since knowledge does not pass over to the *dharma*-s, it is praised as unrelated to any object.

❀ ❀ ❀

IV.97. There is never unrelatedness for one who has the misapprehension that something dharmic, even one the measure of an atom, is born.

❀ ❀ ❀

IV.98. All *dharma*-s are without covering, pure by nature, enlightened from the very beginning (*adi-buddha*), and thus liberated (*mukta*). Those who lead others on the path to salvation (i.e. the *buddha*-s), it is said, know this.

❀ ❀ ❀

IV.100. Having awakened to the state hard to see, very profound, birthless, uniform, free from fear (*visharada*), we honor it to the best of our ability.

Ribhu Gita

I.19. The *Guru*, indeed, does not exist; truly, there is no disciple. There being only *Brahman* alone, be of the certitude that there is no non-Self.

❀   ❀   ❀

I.23. If there is bondage, there is liberation; in the absence of bondage, there is no liberation. If there is death, there is birth; in the absence of birth, there is no death either.

❀   ❀   ❀

I.29. Therefore, all this does not exist in the least at any time: neither you nor I, neither this nor that. There being only *Brahman* alone, be of the certitude that there is no non-Self.

❀   ❀   ❀

I.46. I am the Self, which is *Brahman* alone. I am solely a mass of pure Consciousness. I am the sole-existent, undivided Essence. I am *Brahman* alone.

❀   ❀   ❀

II.23. You alone exist in the kingdom of your Self. You bow only to your own Self. You are of the nature that is full. You are *Brahman*. There is no doubt of this.

II.30. This phenomenal world does not exist. It never was created, nor does it ever exist by itself. This has been called the world-picture; it is ever unreal.

❀   ❀   ❀

III.15. All is illusory. The world is illusory. Likewise are the past, present, and future illusory. Any particular attitude of mind is unreal – utterly unreal. All is illusory. There is no doubt of this.

❀   ❀   ❀

III.44. There is no bondage, but only Consciousness. There is, then, no "Liberation", but only Consciousness. Just Consciousness is the only Reality. This is the Truth, the Truth – I say in the name of Shiva.

❀   ❀   ❀

IV.48. I am liberated from the body and from being the possessor of the body. I am attributeless. I am without "liberation"; I am liberated; I am without [a concept of] liberation, forever.

❀   ❀   ❀

V.15. All bondage, all "liberation", all "knowledge", *Ishvara*, all time, and all instruction are all like the horns of a hare.

❀   ❀   ❀

VI.2. Ribhu: The bath in the Self is the great ablution, the daily ablution. None other is so. This, indeed, is the great ablution: the certitude that I am *Brahman*.

❀   ❀   ❀

VI.57. The mantra "I-am-*Brahman*-I-am" bestows success in the realm of the Self. The mantra "I-am-*Brahman*-I-am" will destroy the unreality.

ॐ

VI.60. Renouncing the seven million great *mantra*-s, which can only confer hundreds of millions of births, one should resort to the *japa* of this one mantra.

❁   ❁   ❁

VII.2. The manifold universe does not exist ever; nor is there anything to be pointed out as "this". There is only *Brahman*, which is ever complete. This is the *tarpana* (libation of water) to *Brahman*.

❁   ❁   ❁

VII.11. All this is only *Brahman*. Nothing else exists anywhere, I affirm. I am That; there is no doubt. This is the *tarpana* to *Brahman*.

❁   ❁   ❁

VII.41. Look upon the *Guru* and the disciple as unreal; then look upon the teachings of the *Guru* also as unreal. Look upon as unreal whatever is an object of perception. This is the rare *homa*.

❁   ❁   ❁

VII.52. All is ever unreal. Existence and creation are unreal. All the *guna*-s are unreal. This is the rare *homa*.

❁   ❁   ❁

VIII.59. I am, indeed, *Brahman*. I am, indeed, *Brahman*. I am, indeed, *Brahman*. It is certain. I am Consciousness. I am Consciousness. One who is thus is called a *jivanmukta*.

❁   ❁   ❁

VIII.61. One who sees only himself in himself, who abides only in himself, and who exists only in his own Self is called a *jivanmukta*.

IX.10. He does not remember himself in the least, anywhere at any time. He who remains in his natural state is the *videhamukta*.

❖ ❖ ❖

IX.12. Remaining silent, silent in all ways, silent in whatever, I am bereft of any purpose. Such is the *videhamukta*.

❖ ❖ ❖

IX.21. All do not exist; only That exists. Just Consciousness exists, ever. The "enlightened one" does not exist. He who is of this conclusion is the *videhamukta*.

❖ ❖ ❖

IX.24. I am *Brahman*. I am all. Nothing else of the world exists. One who has this certitude is the *videhamukta*.

❖ ❖ ❖

IX.54. Blissful in the essence of the Bliss of *Brahman*, ever in the pauseless nectar of *Brahman*, blissful in *Brahman*, and always in Bliss is the *videhamukta*.

❖ ❖ ❖

X.29. Look at the Self alone. Consider yourself to be the Self. Be in your Self. Experience the Self yourself. Nothing exists besides the Self.

❖ ❖ ❖

X.30. Being happy only in one's own Self, considering oneself as the Self, one should perceive oneself as the Self, understanding oneself as the Self.

❖ ❖ ❖

XI.37. All this from beginning to end is unreal. The elite of sages is unreal. The worlds are ever unreal. What is to be seen in the world is unreal.

🕉

XII.29. *Brahman* alone appears as the world and, likewise, as the people. *Brahman* appears as forms. In Reality, there is nothing whatever.

❀ ❀ ❀

XII.56. All states other than *Brahman* are illusory. There is nothing in the least other than *Brahman*. Other than *Brahman*, the world is an illusion. All is only *Brahman* alone.

❀ ❀ ❀

XIII.60. I am only Consciousness. I am only Consciousness, all Consciousness, all Consciousness, ever. True belief is only Consciousness. The conviction of being *Brahman* is only Consciousness.

❀ ❀ ❀

XIV.28. I am the Self, the desirable. This is the truth. This is the truth. This is the truth, again and again. I am the ageless Self, the pervasive. I alone am my own *Guru*.

❀ ❀ ❀

XV.8. Renouncing all, renouncing the *Guru*, and renouncing everything ever, sit in Silence. *Brahman*-Bliss alone exists.

❀ ❀ ❀

XV.22. You yourself are the Space of Consciousness. I am ever the Space of Consciousness. The Space of Consciousness is alone this Consciousness. There is nothing apart from Consciousness-Space.

❀ ❀ ❀

XV.37. The Self alone is the ablution of the Self. The Self alone is the *japa* of the Self. The Self alone is the joy of the Self. The Self alone is the beloved of the Self, ever.

ॐ

XV.54. "All this is *Brahman*; I am He" should be the meditation. All this has been said by the Lord. Be of the certitude that this is so.

❀   ❀   ❀

XVI.24. Ego there is none for me. No sorrow and no faults exist for me. No happiness exists for me. There is no knowledge for me, no thinking for me, no body for me, and no senses for me.

❀   ❀   ❀

XVI.46. All beings are like corpses; all groups are as corpses. The world is ever unreal; all the universe is unreal.

❀   ❀   ❀

XVII.2. Easy is the Knowledge of *Brahman*. It is easy, auspicious, and the best. It is easy for them who are established in *Brahman*, and it gives Knowledge of everything.

❀   ❀   ❀

XVII.37. I am *Brahman* only. "All this" is illusory. I am, indeed, *Brahman*. The world is unreal. I am *Brahman* alone. I am not the body. I am *Brahman* alone, the great Nonduality.

❀   ❀   ❀

XVIII.21. I am *Brahman*, only *Brahman*, and nothing apart from *Brahman*. I am not this, I am not this, I am not this – remember this ever.

❀   ❀   ❀

XVIII.22. I am He-am-I; I am He-am-I; I am *Brahman* – contemplate thus. Consciousness am I; Consciousness am I; I am *Brahman*; Consciousness am I; Consciousness am I – declare thus.

🕉

XVIII.28. Renouncing the renunciation even, ever leave off the idea of any difference. Surrounding your self yourself, abide in your self yourself.

❁ ❁ ❁

XIX.47. Having heard all this about the duality of name and form, all this should be forgotten in a second and abandoned like a scrap of wood or rusted iron.

❁ ❁ ❁

XIX.48. All this is ever unreal, always, like the son of a barren woman. This is just like the horn of a hare. It is just like the horn of a man.

❁ ❁ ❁

XX.11. Some great ignoramuses talk only about duality. They are not fit to be spoken to, not fit to be honored, and not fit to be bowed to.

❁ ❁ ❁

XX.16. The (conceptual) knowledge that duality is real is only due to the intellect of duality. Forget that. All is only *Brahman*; nothing else exists. All is *Brahman* alone.

❁ ❁ ❁

XXI.19. Indescribable, indescribable, I am, indeed, the essence of the Supreme *Brahman*. I am *Brahman*. There is no doubt of this. I am higher than the highest.

❁ ❁ ❁

XXII.49. All is nonexistent, all is nonexistent. I, indeed, am only Consciousness alone. Say so, and stand firm. You shall instantly become liberated.

XXII.51. Firm certitude is, here, the foremost cause. It is this certitude that later becomes natural.

❀ ❀ ❀

XXIII.49. Whoever is devoid of the Knowledge of the Self is, indeed, a great sinner. Whoever is thus devoid of Knowledge is a very sick person, indeed.

❀ ❀ ❀

XXIV.30. It has been said in the scriptures that the world of beings moves by the flow of time and by prescribed rules. This is a mistaken notion, because of the insentience of the world. All this is, on the other hand, by the will of *Ishvara*.

❀ ❀ ❀

XXV.11. Be of the immediate conviction that nothing exists, nothing exists. Be of the conviction that there is nothing to be seen, nothing to be seen, nothing, nothing indeed.

❀ ❀ ❀

XXVI.67. All this is the remnant of thoughts, the muddying of purity. Thus, renouncing all and forgetting everything, like mere dead wood,

❀ ❀ ❀

XXVI.68. Leaving aside the body like a corpse, being ever like a piece of wood or iron, and renouncing even remembrance, firmly abide only in *Brahman* as the goal.

❀ ❀ ❀

XXVII.46. The form of the *jiva*, the concept of *jiva*, the word *jiva* – all these do not exist. The form of *Ishvara*, the concept of *Ishvara*, and the word *Ishvara* are all imagined.

ॐ

XXVIII.42. "Hence, I am, indeed, *Brahman* and all this is false" – thus reflects daily, he who knows *Brahman* best.

❖ ❖ ❖

XXVIII.46. It is declared that "That you are" is the great aphorism of *Upadesha* (instruction). Likewise, "I am *Brahman*" has been defined as an aphorism of experience.

❖ ❖ ❖

XXVIII.47. What arises from the statement "Absolute Knowledge is *Brahman*" is said to be for spiritual exercise, for practice. What arises from the statement "This Self is *Brahman*" is said to be a statement of perception.

❖ ❖ ❖

XXVIII.57. Having reached the state of "I am one with the Supreme", be in your highest, natural state. All "this" is a great illusion, nonexistent, nonexistent. There is no doubt of this.

❖ ❖ ❖

XXIX.15. "Bondage" and "Liberation" are states of the mind. Wherefrom can they arise in its absence? All are illusory. There is no doubt of this. I am *Brahman*. There is no uncertainty in this.

❖ ❖ ❖

XXX.1. I say unto you, there is only the Supreme *Brahman*. This world is not born. I am just the state of Existence, only Bliss. This world is not created.

❖ ❖ ❖

XXX.18. Being of this definite conviction that all is *Brahman*, be happy in the certitude that all is *Brahman*.

XXXI.20. The world would be if a dream object were to continue in the waking state. Let this world ever be if the flowing river stands still.

❖ ❖ ❖

XXXI.23. The world would be if the milk that has been milked out were to flow back again (into the teats) or if there is only a mirror and no reflection.

❖ ❖ ❖

XXXI.28. There is the attitude of duality if there is nescience, action, body, and such. Mind is the mighty disease. If you are afflicted by it, *Brahman* is the physician therefore.

❖ ❖ ❖

XXXII.31. Knowledge is ever pervaded by the Self. I am, indeed, ever the Great. This all is only the Self and nothing else. I am the undivided Self.

❖ ❖ ❖

XXXII.32. If you have this conviction always, you quickly become liberated. You, indeed, are of the nature of *Brahman*. You, indeed, are the embodiment of *Brahman*.

❖ ❖ ❖

XXXII.33. Meditating and meditating thus on the supremely blissful, be happy. All the world is only happiness; the phenomenal world is only love.

❖ ❖ ❖

XXXIII.25. What, indeed, is the Knowledge of the Self? The "I am *Brahman*" certitude is the great upsurge of the Knowledge of the Self.

XXXIII.26. It is the clear perception "I am *Brahman*, I am eternal, I am firmly abiding, I am Bliss – the Supreme Bliss – and I am pure and ever changeless."

❀ ❀ ❀

XXXIII.35. I myself am the *Guru*; I myself am the disciple. Be of this certitude. Though "this" is pointed out, the world, which is limited, never is.

❀ ❀ ❀

XXXIII.37. Being full of this conviction, be happy, released from the body. I am the Self. "This" is nonexistent, as all is only Consciousness.

❀ ❀ ❀

XXXIV.50. This, indeed, is in the heart of the sages. This, indeed, is the exhortation of the gods. This, indeed, is the settled conclusion of all masters – the certitude "I am *Brahman*."

❀ ❀ ❀

XXXIV.51. This is, indeed, the great teaching for all beings for all times. "I am *Brahman*" is the great Liberation. The highest, indeed, is this: I am myself.

❀ ❀ ❀

XXXV.30. There exists no reality or unreality apart from *Brahman*, which transcends the "fourth state". Renouncing all, ever be firmly established in your own Self.

❀ ❀ ❀

XXXVI.37. The unique is *Brahman*. The long-lasting is *Brahman*. All the world is of *Brahman*. *Brahman*, indeed, is *Brahman*. The reality is *Brahman*. Beyond that is *Brahman* only.

🕉

XXXVII.5. There is neither you nor I nor this universe. All is *Brahman* alone. Indeed, there are no beings and no action. All are *Brahman* alone.

❀ ❀ ❀

XXXVII.6. Indeed, there are no deity, no activities, no body, no organs, no wakefulness, no dream, no deep sleep, and no fourth state.

❀ ❀ ❀

XXXVII.7. This universe, indeed, exists not. Be of the certitude that all is *Brahman*. All is illusion, always illusion. Be of the certitude that all is *Brahman*.

❀ ❀ ❀

XXXVII.8. The constant inquiry into *Brahman*, is all *Brahman*, too. Be of this certitude. Likewise, the conviction regarding duality is entirely *Brahman*. Be of this certitude.

❀ ❀ ❀

XXXVIII.40. The word "*Brahman*" exists not, and there is not even the slightest *Brahman-bhava* (conviction about *Brahman*). This text does not exist for me. All exists as *Brahman*.

❀ ❀ ❀

XXXVIII.42. Thus, there is nothing in the least, at any time, anywhere. All is afflictionless Peace. There is only the One and no second. Indeed, there is not even the Oneness.

❀ ❀ ❀

XXXIX.5. The earlier ignorance in my mind has now changed into *Brahman*-hood. Earlier, I was as a being of thought. Now, I am filled with Reality.

XXXIX.6. The earlier attitude of ignorance has now reached the conviction of Reality. I was remaining like ignorance personified. Now, I am *Brahman*. I have reached the Supreme.

❀ ❀ ❀

XXXIX.7. Earlier, I had the misapprehension that I was the mind. Now, I am *Brahman*. I have reached the Supreme. All defects have fled away. All differences have met their dissolution.

❀ ❀ ❀

XXXIX.8. All the universe has fallen off. Thought has entirely gone away. All inner faculties have subsided by the real conviction in *Brahman*.

❀ ❀ ❀

XL.14. My Self is given by myself, abiding fulfilled in itself. You are I, and I am you. Indeed I am you yourself.

❀ ❀ ❀

XL.16. There is, indeed, no place to go. There is nothing else except this identity. There is no place for you or me to go.

❀ ❀ ❀

XL.17. There is only one Cause. There is only One and no second. There is nothing for you to say, and there is nothing more for me to hear.

❀ ❀ ❀

XL.18. You, indeed, are not the revered *Guru*. I am not the disciple. All this is only *Brahman*-ness. I am to be measured by This (*Brahman*-ness), being full of That.

❀ ❀ ❀

XL.21. If I make obeisance to you, you will say I am an ignoramus. If I do it to myself, I become delimited.

ॐ

XL.22. If the prostration is to myself, it is fruitless, being self-centered. There is no prostration to anybody, at any time.

❀ ❀ ❀

XLI.18. I am the universe and the worlds. I am indeed the Self of space. Whatever is conditioned and whatever is unconditioned – all that, indeed, I am.

❀ ❀ ❀

XLII.25. The knower of this treatise is *Brahman*. He becomes *Brahman* himself. What is the need of incessant repetition? This Knowledge confers Liberation.

❀ ❀ ❀

XLIII.13. Acclaim and censure will arise everywhere at all times. By the certitude of each one's own mind, it should be deemed, "I am liberated."

❀ ❀ ❀

XLIII.14. I am, indeed, the Supreme *Brahman*; I am, indeed, the ultimate goal – one who is of this certitude is said to be liberated while alive (*jivan-mukti*).

❀ ❀ ❀

XLIV.13. You have now acquired Knowledge of *Brahman*. You are a blessed soul, indeed. There is no doubt of this. Be ever of the certitude that this is the nature of *Brahman*.

❀ ❀ ❀

XLIV.14. Be of the certitude that there is no liberation other than having this certitude – none other. Certitude is the cause of Liberation. There is no other cause, indeed.

Avadhuta Gita

I.12. Be aware of the *Atman* always. It is continuous and everywhere the same. You say "I am he who meditates", and "The Supreme One is the object of meditation." Why do you thus divide the indivisible?

❈　❈　❈

I.13. You were never born and you will never die. You have neither had a body. The *Upanishad*-s declare in many different ways this avowed truth: "All is *Brahman*."

❈　❈　❈

I.15. For you and me there can be neither union, nor separation. In reality, neither you, nor I, nor this world exists. The *Atman* alone abides.

❈　❈　❈

I.17. You have no birth or death, no memory, no bondage or liberation, nor have you good or evil. Why do you weep, O my dear? Name and form belong neither to you nor to me.

❈　❈　❈

I.23. How can a man attain *samadhi* as long as he thinks of himself as something other than the *Atman*? But, on the other hand, *samadhi* is not possible for a man who thinks of himself as the *Atman*. How can *samadhi* be attained as long as a man thinks that the *Atman* exists and yet does not exist? And what need is there to attain *samadhi* if all are one and by nature free?

✿   ✿   ✿

1.44. I am without beginning, middle, and end. I am never bound. By nature I am pure and perfect – this is my firm conviction.

✿   ✿   ✿

1.56. O mind why do you weep? You are truly the *Atman*. Be one with It. Drink, O my dear, the supreme nectar of the boundless ocean of non-dual *Brahman*.

✿   ✿   ✿

1.58. Sell-knowledge does not depend upon reasoning or the practice of meditation or the instruction of a *guru* or anything in space and time. I am by nature that absolute Knowledge, the Reality, which is innate, eternal, and boundless as space.

✿   ✿   ✿

1.59. I was never born and I will never die. Neither do I perform any action – good or bad. I am that pure, attributeless *Brahman*. How can there be bondage or liberation for me?

✿   ✿   ✿

1.68. My friend mind, what is the use of so much idle talk? My friend mind, all this is a matter of conjecture. I have told you what is the quintessence: You are indeed the Reality – boundless as space.

I.73. The *Avadhuta* lives happily alone in a secluded place, purified by the uninterrupted bliss of *Brahman*. Renouncing the ego, the mendicant *Avadhuta* moves about and finds everything within his own Self.

❀ ❀ ❀

II.1. A *guru* may be young or an enjoyer of worldly pleasures; he may be illiterate or a servant or a householder; but none of these should be taken into consideration. Does one give up a gem dropped in the dirt?

❀ ❀ ❀

II.27. The destiny of the followers of action can be described by the organ of speech, but the goal of the *yogi*-s is inexpressible, because it is not an object to be acquired.

❀ ❀ ❀

II.28. Knowing this, one should not imagine any particular path for the *yogi*-s. They give up desire and doubt, and therefore their perfection takes place spontaneously.

❀ ❀ ❀

II.39. When the *yogi* attains that Supreme *Atman*, he transcends the injunctions and prohibitions of the scriptures. There is no idea of purity or impurity, nor can any evil thought arise in the undifferentiated mind of the *yogi*. Anything forbidden to others is permissible to him because he is beyond all rules.

❀ ❀ ❀

III.3. I am uncreated and separate from creation, for I am ever present. I am unclouded and free from the cloud of *maya*, for I am always manifested. I do not borrow light from another light, and I am also separate from the luminous objects, for I am Self-luminous. I am Existence-Knowledge-Bliss and boundless as space.

ॐ

III.9. I am that fire of knowledge, which consumes all actions of the actionless *Atman*. I am that fire of knowledge, which destroys all sorrows of the sorrowless *Atman*. I am that fire of knowledge which burns up all bodies of the bodiless *Atman*. I am Existence-Knowledge-Bliss and boundless as space.

❀   ❀   ❀

III.34. Why do you weep, my friend? For you there is neither decrepitude nor death; for you there is neither birth nor misery. Why do you weep, my friend? For you there is no disease or modification. I am Existence-Knowledge-Bliss and boundless as space.

❀   ❀   ❀

III.41. Truly, there is no one who meditates within your heart; therefore you have no *samadhi*. There is no meditation within your heart because there is no space without. Indeed, there is no object of meditation within your heart as there is no object or time. I am Existence-Knowledge-Bliss and boundless as space.

❀   ❀   ❀

III.42. I have told you the quintessence of the Supreme Reality. There is neither "you" nor "I" nor superior nor teacher nor disciple. The Ultimate Reality is simple and spontaneous. I am Existence-Knowledge-Bliss and boundless as space.

❀   ❀   ❀

IV.2. *Brahman* is not only free from bondage and liberation, purity and impurity, union and separation, but truly It is ever free. And I am that *Brahman* – infinite as space.

❀   ❀   ❀

IV.19. Know that I am completely absorbed in *Brahman*. Know that I am free from aim and aimlessness. How can I speak of union or separation? I am by nature blissful and free.

ॐ

IV.21. I have no father, no mother, no family; I belong to no race. Never was I born and never shall I die. How can I say that I have affection or delusion? I am by nature blissful and free.

❖ ❖ ❖

IV.24. O my dear, the wise men give up all types of meditation as well as all types of action – good or bad. They drink the nectar of renunciation. I am by nature blissful and free.

❖ ❖ ❖

V.2. The *Upanishad*-s – through their great dictums, such as "Thou art That" and "I am *Brahman*" – have declared that your inmost *Atman* is the Reality. You are the all-embracing Sameness, devoid of all attributes. Being the selfsame *Brahman*, O mind, why do you weep?

❖ ❖ ❖

V.15. *Brahman* pervades equally the open space, the home, and the family. The Supreme Reality has neither attachment nor detachment, neither knowledge nor ignorance. Being the selfsame *Brahman*, O mind, why do you weep?

❖ ❖ ❖

V.23. Bondage and freedom, union and separation, reasoning and inference, and such pairs of opposites, do not converge in *Brahman*. Being the selfsame *Brahman*, O mind, why do you weep?

❖ ❖ ❖

V.28. The all-pervading *Brahman* is free from pleasure and pain, grief and joy. In that Supreme Reality there is no *guru* and no disciple. Being the selfsame *Brahman*, O mind, why do you weep?

🕉

VI.15. It is mere fancy to think that *Brahman* is bound or released, that *Brahman* is created or uncreated. If *Brahman* alone is the indivisible Supreme Beatitude, how can It be either mortal or immortal?

❁   ❁   ❁

VI.22. Look, "you" and "I" have never existed. It is sheer nonsense to consider oneself as having a family or caste. Truly I am *Brahman* – the Supreme Reality. How can I make salutations to It?

❁   ❁   ❁

VII.10. As long as a person has both knowledge and ignorance, and a sense of duality and non-duality, how can he be liberated? Why should one who always enjoys the pure, unadulterated bliss of *Brahman*, and whose innate nature is free from desire and ignorance, try to be a *yogi*?

❁   ❁   ❁

VII.12. Renouncing everything, the *Avadhuta* is always united with *Brahman*. Transcending all elements, he is free. How can there be either life or death for him? What does it matter whether he practices meditation or not?

❁   ❁   ❁

VIII.1. O *Brahman*, by going on a pilgrimage to seek you, I have denied your omnipresence; by meditating on you, I have given you form in my mind and thus denied your formless nature; by singing hymns, I have described you and thus denied your indescribable nature. Forgive me for these three offenses.

Vivekachudamani

4. He is a suicide who has somehow achieved human birth and even manhood and full knowledge of the scriptures but does not strive for self-liberation, for he destroys himself by clinging to the unreal.

❀ ❀ ❀

7. Scripture declares that there is no hope of immortality by means of wealth, so it is evident that liberation cannot be brought about by actions.

❀ ❀ ❀

11. Action is for the purification of the mind, not for the understanding of reality. The recognition of reality is through discrimination, and not by even tens of millions of actions.

❀ ❀ ❀

12. Proper analysis leads to the realization of the reality of the rope, and this is the end of the pain of the fear of the great snake caused by delusion.

❀ ❀ ❀

13. The realization of the truth is seen to depend on meditation on statements about what is good, not on bathing or donations or by hundreds of yogic breathing exercises.

20. *Brahman* is real; the universe is unreal. A firm conviction that this is so is called discrimination between the eternal and the non-eternal.

✿   ✿   ✿

31. Among all means of liberation, devotion is supreme. To seek earnestly to know one's real nature – this is said to be devotion.

✿   ✿   ✿

59. Study of the scriptures is fruitless as long as *Brahman* has not been experienced. And when *Brahman* has been experienced, it is useless to read the scriptures.

✿   ✿   ✿

108. There is One – undifferentiated and undivided. Nobody can define what it is, but it has the power of God. Beginningless and, yet, also called ignorance, it has three qualities: *sattva, rajas,* and *tamas.* It cannot be understood, except by its action, and that, only by the illumined ones. It has created all this universe – produced it all. It is *Maya.*

✿   ✿   ✿

215. You become the witness of that which you see. When there is nothing to be seen, the concept of a witness becomes irrelevant.

✿   ✿   ✿

216. But of one who can never be comprehended – who can be the witness of that? Therefore, the *Atman* is the witness of Himself, because He knows Himself.

✿   ✿   ✿

230. *Brahman,* alone is real, and whatever comes out from *Brahman* is real. The real cannot produce what is unreal. It is

That. There is nothing except That. He that says there is something separate, his delusion has not yet vanished; He is as one speaking in his sleep.

❖ ❖ ❖

231. The supreme scripture of the *Atharva Veda* declares that "All this is *Brahman*", so all this is simply *Brahman*, and anything in addition to that has no reality.

❖ ❖ ❖

232. If it has any reality, that is the end of any eternal reality for oneself, the scriptures are false, and the Lord himself a liar – three things which are quite unacceptable to great souls.

❖ ❖ ❖

234. If the world is real, let it be perceived when you are in deep sleep also. You cannot comprehend anything then. Therefore, it is not. It is like a dream.

❖ ❖ ❖

246. The *Shruti* says, "Not this, not this", because they are attributes and, therefore, not real. As you see the snake in a rope, and as you see things in dream – both unreal – therefore, practice "Not this, not this."

❖ ❖ ❖

256. That which is unaffected by the six afflictions (of aging, death, hunger, thirst, desire and ignorance), which is meditated on in the heart of the devotee, unrecognized by the senses, unknown by the intellect you are That, *Brahman* Himself. Meditate on the fact within yourself.

❖ ❖ ❖

265. Only the consciousness free from all doubts knows that, as the king amongst the soldiers. Taking your stand in that Self always, reduce everything to the *Atman*.

ॐ

293. All that you see is unreal, changing every moment. I cannot be that. I am an unchangeable something. I am the knower of all these changes. There is this awareness in me – that I am the knower of everything. These things (the ego-sense and other perceptions) cannot know anything.

❀ ❀ ❀

320. Reduce the world, which you see, in *Brahman* by thinking of that one Reality, the solidity of all blissfulness; and the internal and the external both being one, think of the blissfulness, pass your time, and be free from all bondage.

❀ ❀ ❀

327. Therefore, with all care, one should try to keep himself recollected and should not be negligent. For the knower of *Brahman*, there is no greater death than this negligence. One who is careful in remaining in *Brahman* becomes successful very soon. Therefore, be careful and stay in *Brahman* all the time.

❀ ❀ ❀

356. So, those who are engaged in *samadhi*, they alone, by reducing the externals (the senses, thought, ego, and all) in Consciousness, being free from the bondage of birth and death, attain the Supreme Bliss – not those who only talk of the *Atman*.

❀ ❀ ❀

364. Hearing of *Brahman* is good, but thinking is one hundred times better than hearing. Millions of times greater than this is meditation. And when one becomes free from doubt in that meditation, that is endlessly greater.

❀ ❀ ❀

369. First, join word with the mind (everything seen is word – names), then mind with the intellect, intellect with ego, ego

ॐ

with the witness, and that witness with *Brahman* who is the Soul of all. And by joining that way, enjoy the eternal Bliss.

❄ ❄ ❄

379. Stop thinking about anything, which is not your true self, for that is degrading and productive of pain, and instead think about your true nature, which is bliss itself and productive of liberation.

❄ ❄ ❄

380. This treasure of consciousness shines unfading with its own light as the witness of everything. Meditate continually on it, making this your aim, distinct as it is from the unreal.

❄ ❄ ❄

391. All this is but Existence Itself, which is beyond word and mind. There is nothing beyond pure existence in what is seen in Nature. Is there anything separate from the earth in the pitcher, jar, etc., which are made from the earth? If anyone says it is separate, he is deluded, like one drunk with the wine of *Maya*. And one drunk with the wine of *Maya* sees "you", "I", etc.

❄ ❄ ❄

396. So long as a man is concerned about the corpse-like body, he is impure and suffers from his enemies in the shape of birth, death and sickness. When however he thinks of himself as pure *Brahman*-like and immovable, then he is freed from those enemies, as the scriptures proclaim.

❄ ❄ ❄

397. Getting rid of all apparent realities within oneself, one is oneself the supreme *Brahman*, perfect, non-dual, and actionless.

ॐ

398. When the mind waves are put to rest in ones true nature, the imageless *Brahman*, then this false assumption exists no longer, but is recognized as just empty talk.

❀   ❀   ❀

403. How can there be distinctions in a supreme reality, which is by nature one? Who has noticed any distinctions in the pure joy of deep sleep?

❀   ❀   ❀

404. After realization of the Supreme Truth, all this no longer exists in one's true nature of the imageless *Brahman*. The snake is not to be found in time, past, present or future, and not a drop of water is to be found in a mirage.

❀   ❀   ❀

413. Like the shadow of a man is this body, which is the result of past actions. Give it up as a corpse, and take no notice of it again, O thou, the great.

❀   ❀   ❀

414. Realize the *Atman*. Pure blissfulness – such is the nature of the *Atman*. Give up this insentient name and form from a distance and never again think of that, as you do not think of food that has been vomited.

❀   ❀   ❀

417. One who has known the true, indivisible Blissfulness in his own Self – really and truly realizing that – for what reason will he support this body?

❀   ❀   ❀

457. So, he who stays in the Supreme always, sees nothing else. Yet, you say he remains in the world. Yes, as is the memory of things seen in dream, so are his actions in this world.

464. Complete in himself, without beginning or end, infinite and unchanging, *Brahman* is one and without a second. There is nothing other than He.

❖ ❖ ❖

465. The essence of Truth, the essence of Consciousness, the eternal essence of Bliss and unchanging, *Brahman* is one and without a second. There is nothing other than He.

❖ ❖ ❖

466. The one reality within everything, complete, infinite, and limitless, *Brahman* is one and without a second. There is nothing other than He.

❖ ❖ ❖

467. He cannot be removed or grasped; he cannot be received from someone else, or held onto. *Brahman* is one and without a second. There is nothing other than He.

❖ ❖ ❖

472. You too should recognize this supreme Truth about yourself, your true nature and the essence of bliss, and shaking off the illusion created by your own imagination, become liberated, fulfilled and enlightened.

❖ ❖ ❖

478. This is the sure decision of Vedanta: *Brahman* is all – the *jiva* and the world. To stay in that state constantly is what is called freedom. And *Brahman* is One without a second. The scripture is the testimony.

❖ ❖ ❖

508. Only fools, when the *upadhi* moves, think that the subject is moving. The subject is actionless like the sun. Only the fools think: "I am the doer and the enjoyer; I am born and I die", etc.

511. Let there be transformations of nature in hundreds, thousands, and millions of ways – what is that to me, who is not attached to them? The clouds never touch the vast sky.

✿ ✿ ✿

515. I am actionless; I am changeless; I am partless; I am without purpose; I am eternal. I do not require any prop. I am One without a second.

✿ ✿ ✿

522. What man of wisdom would abandon the experience of supreme bliss to take pleasure in things with no substance? When the beautiful moon itself is shining, who would want to look at just a painted moon?

✿ ✿ ✿

523. There is no satisfaction or elimination of suffering through the experience of unreal things, so experience that non-dual bliss and remain happily content, established in your own true nature.

✿ ✿ ✿

524. Pass your time, noble one, in being aware of your true nature everywhere, thinking of yourself as non-dual, and enjoying the bliss inherent in yourself.

✿ ✿ ✿

525. Imagining things about the unimaginable and indivisible nature of Awareness is building castles in the sky, so transcending this, experience the supreme peace of silence through your true nature composed of that non-dual bliss.

✿ ✿ ✿

528. He feels delight in his own Self, and; though he may be walking, standing, sitting, or lying on his back, or in any state

whatever, he remains satisfied in his own Self – always thoughtful.

❁ ❁ ❁

530. What discipline is required to recognize that "This is a jar"? All that is necessary is for the means of perception to be in good condition, and if they are, one recognizes the object.

❁ ❁ ❁

531. In the same way this true nature of ours is obvious if the means of perception are present. It does not require a special place or time or purification.

❁ ❁ ❁

532. There are no qualifications necessary to know ones own name, and the same is true for the knower of *Brahman*, knowledge that "I am *Brahman*".

❁ ❁ ❁

537. The child, forgetting hunger and pain, plays with the toys. In like manner, the knower of *Brahman*, forgetting "me" and "mine", rejoices in the *Atman* forever.

❁ ❁ ❁

538. Men of realization live free from preoccupation, eating food begged without humiliation, drinking the water of streams, living freely and without constraint, sleeping in cemetery or forest, their clothing space itself, which needs no care such as washing and drying, the earth as their bed, following the paths of the scriptures, and their sport in the supreme nature of *Brahman*.

❁ ❁ ❁

542. Sometimes he appears like a fool, sometimes like a wise man, sometimes as a king – full of possessions, sometimes as an ignorant man, sometimes quiet, sometimes as that great

snake that attracts with its mesmeric power, sometimes like a worthy man very much respected, sometimes in servitude, sometimes unknown – the wise one wanders thus, always delighted in the Bliss Supreme.

❀   ❀   ❀

555. Just as an actor, whatever his costume may or may not be, is still a man, so the best of men, the knower of *Brahman*, is always *Brahman* and nothing else.

❀   ❀   ❀

566. Like milk poured into milk, oil into oil and water into water, so the ascetic who knows himself becomes united with the One in himself.

❀   ❀   ❀

569. And again, what do you say? This bondage and liberation – they all belong to *Maya*. Virtually they do not exist in the *Atman*; as in the case of the rope – free from change – there is no coming or going of the snake superimposed on the rope.

❀   ❀   ❀

573. Therefore, these two – bondage and freedom – are in *Maya* and not in the *Atman*, which is partless, actionless, quiet, free from impurities, spotless, without defect, and stainless. How can there be any imagination in Him who is non-dual, supreme, and universal like the sky?

❀   ❀   ❀

574. There is no birth, nor death, neither bondage, nor aspirant, neither one desirous of liberation, nor one liberated. This is the Ultimate Truth.

Upadesha Sahasri

I.1.7-8. After teaching these he should teach the definition of *Brahman* through such *Shruti* texts as: "The Self devoid of sins"; "The *Brahman* that is immediate and direct"; "That which is beyond hunger and thirst"; "Not this, not this"; "Neither gross nor subtle"; "This Self is not this"; "It is the Seer Itself unseen"; "Knowledge - Bliss"; "Existence - Knowledge - Infinite"; "Imperceptible bodiless"; "That great unborn Self"; "Without the vital force and the mind"; "Unborn, comprising the interior and exterior"; "Consisting of knowledge only"; "Without interior or exterior"; "It is verily beyond what is know as also what is unknown"; and "Called *Akasha* (the self-effulgent One)", and also through such *Smriti* texts as the following: "It is neither born nor dies"; "It is not affected by anybody's sins"; "Just as air is always in the ether"; "The individual Self should be regarded as the universal one"; "It is called neither existent nor non-existent"; "As the Self is beginningless and devoid of qualities"; "The same in all beings"; and "The Supreme Being is different" – all these support the definition given by the *Shruti* and prove that the innermost Self is beyond transmigratory existence and that it is not different from *Brahman*, the all-comprehensive principle.

ॐ

I.1.37-38. Therefore you are not different from the Supreme Self in as much as you are devoid of impurities such as the connection with the impressions of colors and the like. As there is no contradiction to perceptional evidence etc., the Supreme Self should be accepted as one's self according to the *Shruti*-s: "It knew the pure Self to be *Brahman*"; "It should be regarded as homogeneous"; "It is I that am below"; "It is the Self that is below"; "He knows everything to be the Self"; "When everything becomes the Self"; "All this verily is the Self"; "He is without parts"; "Without the interior and exterior"; "Unborn, comprising the interior and the exterior"; "All this verily is *Brahman*"; "It entered through this door"; "The names of pure knowledge"; "Existence, Knowledge, Infinite *Brahman*"; "From It"; "It created and entered it"; "The shining One without a second, concealed in all beings and all-pervading"; "In all bodies, Itself bodiless"; "It is not born and does not die"; "(Knowing) dream and waking"; "He is my Self, thus one should know"; "Who (knows) all beings"; "It moves and moves not"; "Knowing It, one becomes worthy of being worshipped"; "It and nothing but It is fire"; "I became Manu and the sun"; "Entering into them He rules all creatures"; "Existence only, my child"; and "That is real, That is the Self, thou art That". It is established, that you, the Self, are the Supreme *Brahman*, the One only and devoid of every phenomenal attribute, from the *Smriti* also, such as: "All beings are the body of One who resides in the hearts of all"; "Gods are verily the Self"; "In the city of nine gates"; "The same in all beings"; "In a *Brahmana* wise and courteous"; "Undivided in things divided"; and "All this verily is *Vasudeva* (the Self)".

❀   ❀   ❀

I.2.109. Disciple: – "Sir, if this is so, independent of evidences regarding Itself, eternal and changeless knowledge, which is the Consciousness of the Self, is surely self-evident, and all things different from It, and therefore non-conscious, have an existence only for the sake of the Self as they combine to act for another (in order that the events of the universe may continue uninterruptedly). It is only as the knowledge of the mental modifications giving rise to pleasure, pain and delusion that the non-Self serves the purpose of another. And it is as the same knowledge and as nothing else that it has an existence. Just as a rope-snake, the water in a mirage and such other things are found to be non-existent except only the knowledge by which they are known; so, the duality experienced during waking and dream has reasonably no existence except the knowledge by which it is known. So, having a continuous existence, Pure Consciousness, the Self, is eternal and immutable, and never ceasing to exist in any mental modification. It is one without a second. The modifications themselves cease to exist, the Self continuing to do so. Just as in dream the mental modifications appearing to be blue, yellow, etc., are said to be really non-existent as they cease to exist while the knowledge by which they are known has an uninterrupted continuous existence; so, in the waking state also they are reasonably really non-existent, as they cease to exist while the very same knowledge continues to do so. As that knowledge has no other knower, it cannot be accepted or rejected by Itself. As there is nothing else (except Myself, the aim of my life is fulfilled by your grace)."

❀ ❀ ❀

I.2.110. Teacher: – "It is exactly so. It is Ignorance due to which the transmigratory existence consisting of waking and dream is experienced. It is Knowledge that brings this Ignorance to end. You have thus attained Fearlessness. You will never again feel pain in waking or in dream. You are liberated from the misery of this transmigratory existence.

❀ ❀ ❀

II.1.15. It is, therefore, not possible on the part of a man of knowledge to have Knowledge and perform an action at the same time as they are incompatible with each other. So, one who aspires after liberation should renounce actions.

ॐ

II.2.1. Impossible "to be negated", the Self is left over on the authority of the *Shruti* "Not this, not this!". So, the Self becomes clearly known on the reflection, "I am not this, I am not this!"

❀   ❀   ❀

II.2.3. A following knowledge does not arise without negating the previous one (e.g. the knowledge of the rope does not come without destroying that of the snake in a rope-snake). Pure Consciousness, the Self, only has an independent existence and is never negated as It is the result of evidences.

❀   ❀   ❀

II.5.1. People do not receive Self-knowledge on account of the fear that their duties (according to their castes and orders of life) would be destroyed, like Udanka who did not accept genuine nectar which, he thought, was urine.

❀   ❀   ❀

II.10.3. I am unborn, deathless, devoid of old age, immortal, self-effulgent, all-pervading, and non-dual. Perfectly pure, having neither cause nor effect and contended with the one Bliss, I am free. Yes.

❀   ❀   ❀

II.10.6. But it is true that I have no change nor any cause of a change, as I am without a second. As I do not possess a body, I have neither sin nor virtue, neither bondage nor liberation, neither a caste nor an order of life.

❀   ❀   ❀

II.11.2. The scriptures negate Vedic actions with their accessories by saying, "Knowledge alone is the cause of immortality", and that "there is nothing else to co-operate with it (in producing liberation)".

🕉

II.11.15. As actions have Ignorance for their cause, there is no hope from them of immortality. As liberation is caused by right Knowledge (alone), it does not depend on anything else.

❖ ❖ ❖

II.12.4. Say how there can reasonably be the two contrary ideas "You do this" and "You are *Brahman*" at the same time and in respect of the same person.

❖ ❖ ❖

II.12.17. Agency depends on doership, instruments, etc., but non-agency is natural. It has been therefore, very well ascertained that the knowledge that one is a doer and experiencer is certainly false.

❖ ❖ ❖

II.14.13. A knower of the Self will wish to perform actions if one who has reached the other bank of a river wishes to reach that bank while there.

❖ ❖ ❖

II.14.16. The Self whose Consciousness never ceases to exist neither remembers nor forgets Itself. That the mind remembers the Self is also a knowledge caused by Ignorance.

❖ ❖ ❖

II.14.23. Be in peace. What is the use of efforts if the Self has been known to be naturally free from the ideas "me" and "mine" and from efforts and desires?

❖ ❖ ❖

II.14.39. Always meditating on the Self, one has nothing to do with time etc., as the Self is in no way connected with time, space, direction and causation.

ॐ

II.15.1. As one cannot become another, one should not consider *Brahman* to be different from oneself. For if one becomes another, one is sure to be destroyed.

✿ ✿ ✿

II.15.6. As it is said in the *Shruti*, pleasure and pain (do not touch one who is bodiless). Bodilessness is not the result of actions. The cause of our connection with a body is action. Therefore, an aspirant after knowledge should renounce actions.

✿ ✿ ✿

II.16.18. Transmigratory existence consists of waking and dream. Their root is deep sleep consisting of Ignorance. No one of these three states has a real existence because each goes out of existence when another remains in it. One should, therefore, give up all these three states.

✿ ✿ ✿

II.16.39-41. Liberation becomes artificial and therefore transitory according to the philosopher who holds that it is a change of one state into another on the part of the Self. Again it is not reasonable that it is a union (with *Brahman*) or a separation (from Nature). As both union and separation are transitory, Liberation cannot consist of the individual Self going to *Brahman* or of *Brahman* coming to it. But the Self, one's own real nature, is never destroyed. For, It is uncaused and cannot be accepted or rejected by oneself (or by others), while other things (e.g. states, etc.) are caused.

✿ ✿ ✿

II.16.57. There is no bondage in the Self as there is no change of condition in It. There is no impurity in the Self inasmuch as It is "unattached", as the *Shruti* says.

ॐ

II.17.6. Of the nature of being always attained, the Self does not depend on anything else in order to be acquired. The acquisition that depends on other things (e.g. effort, etc.) is due to Ignorance (and so vanishes when the means to which it is due vanish).

❁ ❁ ❁

II.17.20. Unperceived in deep sleep but perceived (in waking and dream) by those only who are ignorant, the whole of this universe is an outcome of Ignorance and therefore unreal.

❁ ❁ ❁

II.17.49. The outcome of the ascertainment of the real nature of the Self is cessation from actions, etc. The Self is neither an end nor a means. It is, according to the *Smriti*, eternally contented.

❁ ❁ ❁

II.17.50. Four things only are the results of actions, viz., the production, acquisition, transformation, and purification, of something. They produce no other results. All actions with their accessories should therefore, be given up.

❁ ❁ ❁

II.17.64. Whom should the knower of the Self salute if he is established in his own Glory which is infinite, non-dual, and beyond name, etc.? Actions then have no utility for him.

❁ ❁ ❁

II.17.83. The Self cannot be accepted or rejected by Itself or others, nor does It accept or reject anyone else. This is right Knowledge.

❁ ❁ ❁

II.18.3. If the conviction, "I am nothing but Existence and am ever free" were impossible to be attained, why should the *Shruti* teach us that, so affectionately like a mother?

II.18.95. All this non-Self exists only for those people who are discriminating, but it does not exist at all for men of Knowledge.

❖ ❖ ❖

II.18.159. It is to the intellect and not to the Self which is immutable that the knowledge "I am *Brahman*" belongs. Moreover, the Self is changeless because It has no other witness.

❖ ❖ ❖

II.18.180. The method of agreement and contrariety is spoken of in order that one may be acquainted with the (implied) meanings of words. For no one can know the meaning of a sentence without knowing (the meaning of the words in it).

❖ ❖ ❖

II.18.190-191. It is from the sentence only and from nothing else that one knows oneself to be ever free. The meaning of the sentence is known from the knowledge of the (implied) meanings of the words; these meanings again are surely understood by the method of agreement and contrariety. Thus one knows oneself to be free from pain and action.

❖ ❖ ❖

II.18.209. Knowing that one is eternally existing Liberation, one who desires to perform actions is a man of clouded intellect and nullifies the scriptures.

❖ ❖ ❖

II.18.210. For knowing oneself to be *Brahman* one has no duty to perform; nor can one be a knower of *Brahman* when one has duties to perform. One deceives oneself by having recourse to both sides.

II.18.226-227. That one is *Brahman* is the right knowledge. It is not negated by the false conceptions that one is an agent, has desires and is bound, arising from fallacious evidences. This (false) knowledge (i.e. "I am an agent") like the identification of the Self with the body, becomes unreasonable when the knowledge that one is *Brahman* and not other than It is firmly grasped according to the teaching of the scriptures.

❀ ❀ ❀

II.19.8. Scrutinized through the reasoning that reality is never destroyed and unreality never born, you have no (real) existence. You are, therefore, Oh my mind, non-existent in the Self. Having both, birth and death, you are accepted as non-existent.

Aparokshanubhuti

5. *Atman* in itself is alone permanent; the "seen" is opposed to it, such a settled conviction is truly known as discrimination.

❖ ❖ ❖

9. "Oh! Ocean of Mercy, how can the liberation from this world and its bondage come to me?" – such deep desire for liberation is termed *Mumukshutva*.

❖ ❖ ❖

12. Who am I? How is this world created? Who is the creator? What is the material cause for this? This is the way of enquiry.

❖ ❖ ❖

27. I am without any qualities, and actionless, eternal and ever liberated, and I am immutable. And I am not the body, which is unreal. This is known as real Knowledge by the wise.

❖ ❖ ❖

29. O Fool! Why do you imagine that the Self which is accepted (by *Shruti*) as *Purusha*, the Auspicious, which is in and yet beyond the body, to be a mere void and non-existent?

45. The substratum for the whole universe is nothing but *Brahman*. Therefore, the whole universe is *Brahman* and nothing else.

❁ ❁ ❁

47. *Shruti*, by its own direct statements has totally negated the multiplicity of the universe. When the Non-dual cause is thus an established fact how can there be anything other than That?

❁ ❁ ❁

50. The *Shruti* declares that *Brahman* alone shines as different names and forms. All activities are nothing but *Brahman*.

❁ ❁ ❁

67. When a pot is seen, in fact it is the mud alone we are perceiving, so too when we observe the world, it is the ever-effulgent *Brahman* that is seen (in and through the objects).

❁ ❁ ❁

68. Just as a rope is seen differently, as a rope or as a snake, so also the Self, which is ever-pure, is seen differently, by the wise as Pure, and by the ignorant as impure (world of objects).

❁ ❁ ❁

72. Gold is mistaken for an earring, water of the ocean is perceived as waves; so too the ignorant has mistaken the *Atman* as the body.

❁ ❁ ❁

89. Oh! Most Intelligent One, spend your time in realizing the Self at all times. While experiencing the fruits of past actions, you need not be anxious of anything.

91. Just as the dream is unreal for the waker, so too after realization, the bodies are unreal and therefore there is no *Prarabdha*.

❁   ❁   ❁

92. The actions of the previous (other) births are known as *Prarabdha*. For the realized, there is no question of other births, so the "*Prarabdha*" also does not exist.

❁   ❁   ❁

113. That which is famously known as the beginning of all beings, that which is the immutable substratum for the entire work of happenings. That, in which the men of realization, stay merged. That is to be understood as "*Siddhasan*".

❁   ❁   ❁

119-120. The negation of the world of plurality is to be considered as "*Rechaka*" (breathing out), continuous thought of "I am *Brahman*" is called "*Puraka*" (breathing in), and the steadiness in that thought thereafter is called "*Kumbhaka*" (holding the breath within). This is true "*Pranayama*" to the wise, while the ignorant merely tortures his nose.

❁   ❁   ❁

121. To dissolve the mind in the Consciousness, knowing the expression of one's Self in all the objects is known as "*Pratyahara*". This should be practiced by all the seekers diligently.

❁   ❁   ❁

122. On whatever object the mind may fall, having the vision of *Brahman* to steady the mind, this is known as "*Dharana*", and this is the highest concentration.

123. By constant knowledge that "I am *Brahman*", not to rest on anything for any support is known by the term "*Dhyana*", and this is the bestower of Supreme Bliss.

❁   ❁   ❁

129. By thinking of any object the mind will be full of That alone. By thinking of void, the mind will be void. By entertaining the thoughts of *Brahman,* the mind also will be full of That alone. Therefore, one should think of *Brahman* alone always.

❁   ❁   ❁

142. Merging the manifest into the unmanifest, meditating that everything is *Brahman*, the wise seeker should rest blissfully in the state of Absolute Awareness.

Atmabodha

3. Action cannot remove ignorance for they are not opposed. Self-Knowledge removes it as light removes darkness.

❁　❁　❁

9. The world of animate and inanimate objects is projected by imagination on the all-pervading substratum.

❁　❁　❁

10. Just as bracelets, bangles, and rings are gold in various forms, the forms in this world are nothing but Awareness.

❁　❁　❁

11. Space seems broken and diverse because of the many forms in it. Remove the forms and pure space remains. So too with the omnipresent Self.

❁　❁　❁

27. As a lamp illumines objects in a room, the Self illumines the mind, which is composed of inert subtle matter and unable to illumine itself.

❁　❁　❁

28. One lamp is not needed to illumine the light of another. A

second awareness is not needed to know the Self, Pure Awareness.

❖ ❖ ❖

29. Negating the conditionings with the knowledge "I am not this" realize your Self identity as indicated in scripture.

❖ ❖ ❖

33. Scripture says I am pure, without thought and desire, and so I am.

❖ ❖ ❖

34. I have no attributes. I live without breathing. I am eternal, formless, and ever-free.

❖ ❖ ❖

36. The impression "I am the Self" created by constant practice destroys ignorance and agitation just as medicine destroys disease.

❖ ❖ ❖

43. Though an ever-present reality, the Self is not realized due to ignorance. Its realization is like the discovery of a lost object.

❖ ❖ ❖

45. The ignorance "I" and "mine" are removed by Self-Knowledge, just as right information removes wrong knowledge about directions.

❖ ❖ ❖

47. The Self alone exists. The physical universe is the Self. As pots made of clay are nothing but clay, everything is the Self to the enlightened.

52. When conditionings dissolve, the enlightened are absorbed into the all-pervading Reality, like water into water and light into light.

❁ ❁ ❁

53. Realize that to be the Self, the attainment of which leaves nothing to be attained, the blessedness of which leaves no blessings to be desired, the knowledge of which leaves nothing more to be known.

❁ ❁ ❁

63. All that is perceived or heard is the Self. Knowing the Self, one sees everything as Reality, non-dual Being, absolute Bliss, pure Awareness.

Dakshinamurti Stotra

1. Atman as the Ego

To Him who by illusion of *Atman*, as by sleep, sees the universe existing within Himself – like a city seen to exist within a mirror – as though it were manifested without; to Him who beholds, when awake, His own very Self, the secondless; to Him who is incarnate in the Teacher; to Him in the Effulgent Form Facing the South; to Him (*Shiva*) be this bow!

❊   ❊   ❊

2. Atman as the First Cause

To Him who, like unto a magician, or even like unto a mighty *Yogin*, displays by His own will this universe, undifferentiated in the beginning like the plant within the seed, but made afterwards picturesque in all its variety in combination with space and time created by *Maya*; to Him who is incarnate in the Teacher; to Him in the Effulgent Form Facing the South; to Him (*Shiva*) be this bow!

ॐ

3. Unity of Atman

To Him in the Effulgence Form Facing the South, whose light, which is Existence itself, shines forth entering the objects which are almost non-existent; to Him incarnate, in the *Guru* who instructs the disciples in the Vedic text "That thou art"; to Him who being realized there will be no more return to the ocean of *samsara*; to Him (*Shiva*) be this bow!

❀   ❀   ❀

4. Atman the One Existence and Light

All this world shines after Him alone shining in the consciousness "I know", – after Him alone whose consciousness, luminous like the light of a mighty lamp standing in the bosom of a many-holed pot, moves outwards through the sense-organs such as the eye. To Him who is incarnate in the Teacher; to Him in the Effulgent Form Facing the South; to Him (*Shiva*) be this bow!

❀   ❀   ❀

5. False Personations of Atman

Those who contend that the Ego is the body, or the vitality, or the sense-organs, or the fickle *buddhi*, or the void, they are verily on the same level with women and children, with the blind and the possessed; they are quite deluded. To Him who destroys the mighty delusion set up by the play of *Maya's* power; to Him who is incarnate in the Teacher; to Him in the Effulgent Form Facing the South; to Him (*Shiva*) be this bow!

🕉

6. Atman the Eternal Existence

To the *Atman* who, going to *sushupti* on the withdrawal of sense-organs, becomes the One Existence, enshrouded by *Maya* like unto the sun or moon in eclipse, and whose then existence is recognized on waking in the consciousness "I have slept till now"; to Him who is incarnate in the Teacher; to Him in the Effulgent Form Facing the South; to Him (*Shiva*) be this bow!

❂   ❂   ❂

7. Atman the Eternal Light

To Him who, by means of the blessed symbol, manifests to the disciples the True Self that always shines within as the Ego, constant in all the varying states of infancy, (manhood, and old age), of *jagrat* (*svapna and sushupti*) and so on; to Him who is incarnate in the Teacher; to Him in the Effulgent Form Facing the South; to Him (*Shiva*) be this bow!

❂   ❂   ❂

8. Maya

To the *Atman* who, deluded by *Maya*, sees, in *jagrat* or *svapna*, the universe in variety, as cause and effect, as master and servant, as teacher and disciple, as father and son, and so on ; to Him who is incarnate in the Teacher; to Him in the Effulgent Form Facing the South; to Him (*Shiva*) be this bow !

ॐ

9. Devotion to Ishvara

To Him whose eightfold body is all this moving and unmoving universe, appearing as earth, water, fire, air, space, the sun, the moon, and soul – beyond whom, supreme and all-pervading, there exists none else for those who investigate; to Him who is incarnate in the Teacher; to Him in the Effulgent Form Facing the South; to Him (*Shiva*) be this bow!

❖   ❖   ❖

10. Perfection

Because the universality of *Atman* has thus been explained in this hymn, therefore by hearing it, by reflecting and meditating upon its teaching, and by reciting it, that Divine State which is endued with the mighty grandeur of being the Universal Self shall, of itself, come into being, as also that unimpeded Divine Power presenting itself in forms eight.

Bhaja Govindam

1. Adore the Lord, adore the Lord, adore the Lord, Oh fool! When the appointed time (for departure) comes, the repetition of grammar rules will not save you. (Seek Govind, Seek Govind...).

❖ ❖ ❖

2. Oh fool! Leave off the desire for accumulation of wealth; create in the mind thoughts about Reality, devoid of passion. What you get i.e., what you have achieved through your past deeds – with that, satisfy your mind. (Seek Govind, Seek Govind...).

❖ ❖ ❖

3. Seeing the seductive female form, do not fall prey to frenzied delusion. That (female form) is (but) a modification of flesh and fat. Think well thus in your mind again and again. (Seek Govind, Seek Govind...).

❖ ❖ ❖

4. The water on the lotus-leaf is very unsteady; so also is life extremely unstable. Know that the entire world is devoured by disease and conceit, and smitten with sorrow. (Seek Govind, Seek Govind...).

5. As long as you have the ability to earn money, so long will your dependents be attached to you. After that, when you live with an infirm body, no one would even speak to you a word. (Seek Govind, Seek Govind…).

❖ ❖ ❖

7. When a boy, one is attached to sport; when a youth, one is attached to a young woman; when old, one is attached to anxiety; To the Supreme *Brahman*, no one, alas, is attached! (Seek Govind, Seek Govind…).

❖ ❖ ❖

8. Who is your wife? Who is your son? Exceedingly wonderful, indeed, is this empirical process! Of whom are you? Who are you? Whence have you come? Oh brother, think of that truth here. (Seek Govind, Seek Govind…).

❖ ❖ ❖

9. Through the company of the good, there arises non-attachment; through non-attachment there arises freedom from delusion; through delusionlessness, there arises steadfastness; through steadfastness, there arises liberation in life. (Seek Govind, Seek Govind…).

❖ ❖ ❖

10. When youth is spent, what lustful play is there? When the water has evaporated, what lake is there? When the money is gone, what dependents are there? When the Truth is known, what empirical process is there? (Seek Govind, Seek Govind…).

❖ ❖ ❖

11. Do not be proud of wealth, kindred and youth; time takes away all these in a moment. Leaving aside this entire (World) which is of the nature of an illusion, and knowing the state of *Brahman*, enter into it. (Seek Govind, Seek Govind…).

12. Day and night, dusk and dawn, winter and spring come repeatedly; time sports, life is fleeting; yet one does not leave the winds of desire. (Seek Govind, Seek Govind...).

❁ ❁ ❁

13. Why worry about wife, wealth, etc., Oh crazy one; is there not for you the One who ordains? In these three worlds, it is only the association with good people that can serve as the boat that can carry one across the sea of birth. (Seek Govind, Seek Govind...).

❁ ❁ ❁

14. The ascetic with matted locks, the one with his head shaven, the one with hairs pulled out one by one, the one who disguises himself variously with the ochre-colored robes; such a one is a fool, who, though seeing, does not see. Indeed, this varied disguise is for the sake of the belly. (Seek Govind, Seek Govind...).

❁ ❁ ❁

15. The body has become decrepit; the head has turned grey; the mouth has been rendered toothless; grasping a stick, the old man moves about. Even then, the mass of desires does not go! (Seek Govind, Seek Govind...).

❁ ❁ ❁

16. In front, there is fire; at the back, there is the sun; in the night, (the ascetic sits) with the knees stuck to the chin; he receives alms in his palms, and lives under the trees; yet the bondage of desire does not leave him. (Seek Govind, Seek Govind...).

❁ ❁ ❁

17. One goes on pilgrimage to the place where the Ganga joins the sea; or observes the religious vows with care; or offers

gifts. But if he be devoid of knowledge, he does not gain release – according to all schools of thought – even in a hundred lives. (Seek Govind, Seek Govind...).

❀ ❀ ❀

19. Let one practice concentration; or let one indulge in sense-enjoyment. Let one find pleasure in company; or in solitude. He alone is happy, happy, verily happy, whose mind revels in *Brahman*. (Seek Govind, Seek Govind...).

❀ ❀ ❀

22. He who wears a dress made of rags that lie about in the streets, he who walks the path that is beyond merit and demerit, the *Yogin* whose mind is given up to Yoga revels (in *Brahman*) just as a child or as a mad-man. (Seek Govind, Seek Govind...).

❀ ❀ ❀

23. Who are you? Who am I? Whence have I come? Who is my mother? Who is my father? Thus enquire, leaving aside the entire world which is comparable to a dream, and is essenceless. (Seek Govind, Seek Govind...).

❀ ❀ ❀

26. Leaving off egocentric desire, anger, greed and delusion, make self-inquiry: Who am I? They are fools who are without Self-knowledge; as captives in Hell, they are tortured. (Seek Govind, Seek Govind...).

❀ ❀ ❀

28. One easily takes to carnal enjoyment; afterwards, lo, there is disease of the body. Although, in the world, death is the refuge, even then one does not relinquish sinful ways. (Seek Govind, Seek Govind...).

29. Wealth is not good: thus reflect always. There is not the least happiness therefrom: this is the truth. For the wealthy, there is fear even from the son; everywhere this is the regular mode. (Seek Govind, Seek Govind...).

❁   ❁   ❁

31. Being devoted completely to the lotus-feet of the Master, become released soon from the transmigratory process. Thus, through the discipline of sense and mind-control, you will behold the Deity that resides in your heart. (Seek Govind, Seek Govind...).

Amritanubhava

I.18. Two sticks produce only one sound, two flowers (of the same tree) only one fragrance, two lamps only one light.

❀   ❀   ❀

I.19. Two lips utter only one word, two eyes give only one vision – likewise even though they seem to be two they are only one pervading the universe. (In effect, they are one and the same).

❀   ❀   ❀

III.19. Should the knowledge of the (Self), which is all pure, need the support of another knowledge (to know)? Would it not be like the sun depending on another's strength (to shine)?

❀   ❀   ❀

III.21. Is it ever possible that anyone, not knowing that he is with himself will find himself out by wandering from country to country?

❀   ❀   ❀

V.1. The Supreme (*Sat-Cit-Ananda*) is a triad of existence, knowledge and bliss; however, understand that they are missing in it: like the poison is not in the poison.

V.8. The sixteen phases of the moon go on waxing during the first fortnight (of the lunar month); yet the moon is as it is, in itself a perfect whole.

❀ ❀ ❀

V.9. When rainwater is falling in drops, it could be counted by drops; however, on the spot where it falls, it is all water only (it cannot be counted there).

❀ ❀ ❀

V.13. Thus the word "*Sat-Cit-Ananda*" as applied to *Atman* (the Self) does not really represent it. It is to establish its differentiation from other attributes such as "*asat*", "*jada*" and "*dukha*" (i.e. non-existence, grossness and misery).

❀ ❀ ❀

V.26. Whatever is said about it (the Supreme), it is not that; and whatever it is, cannot be said; it is the way one cannot measure one's height by measuring one's shadow;

❀ ❀ ❀

V.45. (Or) when the moon is in the sky at noontime the existence of moonlight can be known by the moon only.

❀ ❀ ❀

V.50. Those who can enjoy the beauty of their face without the aid of the mirror can alone realize the secrets of the self-evident Supreme.

❀ ❀ ❀

VI.20. One who says that the word destroys ignorance and that the *Atman* reveals itself would be (labeled as having gone) mad.

ॐ

VI.41. It is not a finding of the intellect that the *Atman* destroys ignorance and reveals himself. He is like the sun who has no darkness (to destroy before revealing himself).

❀ ❀ ❀

VI.55. To what extent to expatiate on this subject? The ignorance is made up of non-existence; how can it be destroyed by words?

❀ ❀ ❀

VI.97. The ignorance being non-existent, it cannot be destroyed; and the *Atman* being self-evident, what is there to be established and by whom?

❀ ❀ ❀

VII.3. As dream's greatness lies in dream; darkness is recognized in darkness; so is the greatness of ignorance in ignorance only.

❀ ❀ ❀

VII.54. So, when it (ignorance) has not allowed any proof to exist and there is no one to take its brief, from this discussion realize that ignorance is false.

❀ ❀ ❀

VII.55. Thus the ignorance being incapable of being established directly (by proof) or indirectly by inference, stands disproved.

❀ ❀ ❀

VII.84. By all means we really tried to bring out ignorance. But it does not exist. How long we should go on saying this!

🕉

VII.214. Does the face become of no avail if it does not see itself in a mirror? Even without a mirror it is in itself.

✿ ✿ ✿

VII.215. In that way, if *Maya* (ignorance) does not show *Atman* to *Atman* then who will be of no avail, the *Atman* or *Maya*?

✿ ✿ ✿

VII.252. Here neither the words are tolerated, nor is the knowledge accommodated, nor the experience permitted to parade itself.

✿ ✿ ✿

VII.253. Therefore, his seeing himself is like this. In fact no one sees anything.

✿ ✿ ✿

VII.254. What is more! The *Atman* illumines on account of the *Atman* only and he remains awake without being awakened.

✿ ✿ ✿

VII.260. In that way, the *Atman* never misses his own self, whatever role as per his own liking he may assume out of fun.

✿ ✿ ✿

VIII.7. There is no wonder; we can neither reveal nor conceal ourselves. Our state of existence somehow survives.

✿ ✿ ✿

VIII.18. The one who knows, knows not; and one who does not know, knows. What is the use of continuing such existence by knowledge and ignorance?

ॐ

IX.66. Oh! You have awakened the already awake, lulled to sleep the one already asleep, and brought to us ourselves (made us realize ourselves). What a wonder of yours!

❀ ❀ ❀

X.8. Whatever we have spoken is apparent by itself. Does the self-illumined (Supreme) need words to enlighten Itself?

❀ ❀ ❀

X.11. There is no other mystery about the Pure Consciousness than this: It has already been there even before it was enunciated.

Panchadasi

I.53. The finding out or discovery of the true significance of the identity of the individual self and the Supreme with the aid of the great sayings (*Mahavakya*-s) is what is known as *Shravana*. And to arrive at the possibility of its validity through logical reasoning is what is called *Manana*.

✿ ✿ ✿

I.54. And, when by *Shravana* and *Manana* the mind develops a firm and undoubted conviction, and dwells constantly on the thus ascertained Self alone, it is called *Nididhyasana* (unbroken meditation).

✿ ✿ ✿

III.19. How can a man teach scriptures to one who is a man only in form but who is so dull as not to experience what consciousness is in every act of knowing a thing?

✿ ✿ ✿

III.20. As it is shameful for a man to express doubt if he has a tongue or not, so also it is shameful to say, "I do not know what consciousness is, I must know it now."

VI.12. Therefore one should always enquire into the nature of the world, the individual Self and the Supreme Self. When the ideas of *jiva* and *jagat* (world) are negated, the pure *Atman* alone remains.

❀ ❀ ❀

VI.130. *Maya* is looked upon in three ways. From the point of view of knowledge and *Shruti* it is negligible; for empirical reason it is indefinable (*anirvachaniya*); and for the ordinary people it is real.

❀ ❀ ❀

VI.139. *Maya* is an embodiment of marvellousness and doubt; the wise must carefully find out means and make effort to remove it.

❀ ❀ ❀

VI.134. Without in anyway affecting the real nature of *Atman*, *Maya* creates the world. It makes the impossible look possible. How astonishingly powerful *Maya* is!

❀ ❀ ❀

VI.214. Those who do not know the nature of *Brahman*, who is secondless and associationless, fruitlessly quarrel over *jiva* and *Ishvara*, which are creations of *Maya*.

❀ ❀ ❀

VII.20. When a man is as firmly convinced of his identity with *Brahman* as an ordinary man is convinced of his identity with the body, he is liberated even if he does not wish for it.

❀ ❀ ❀

VII.22. The Self is ever cognized. We speak of Its being known directly or indirectly, being known or unknown, as in the illustration of the tenth man.

ॐ

VII.23. The tenth man counts the other nine, each of whom is visible to him, but forgets himself the tenth, though all the time sees himself.

❖ ❖ ❖

VII.28. Seven stages can be distinguished in respect of the Self: (1) Ignorance, (2) Obscuration, (3) Superimposition, (4) Indirect Knowledge, (5) Direct Knowledge, (6) Cessation of Grief and (7) the Rise of Perfect Satisfaction.

❖ ❖ ❖

VII.61. The Vedic texts, such as "Before the creation *Brahman* alone existed", give indirect knowledge of *Brahman*; but the text "That thou art" gives direct knowledge.

❖ ❖ ❖

VII.75. The relation between the two substantives ("thou" and "that") should not be taken as that of one qualifying the other or of mutual qualification, but of complete identity, of absolute homogeneity. That is the meaning of the expression, according to competent persons: what is "thou" is wholly and fully "that", and what is "that" is wholly and fully "thou" – both the terms indicate absolute homogeneous consciousness.

❖ ❖ ❖

VII.99. The causes of the lack of firmness in the direct knowledge of *Brahman* are: (1) the occurrence of apparently contradictory texts, (2) the doubt about the possibility of such a knowledge and (3) radically opposed ways of thinking leading to the idea of doership.

❖ ❖ ❖

VII.106. The practice of meditation on *Brahman*, the wise consider, means reflection on It, talking about It, mutually producing logical arguments about It – thus to be fully occupied with it alone.

🕉

VII.107. The wise man, having known *Brahman* beyond doubt, ought to generate a flow of unbroken thought-current on It. He should not engage in much discussion, for that has but one effect – it tires the organ of speech.

❁　❁　❁

VII.139. Wealth brings worry in earning, anxiety in maintenance, grief in loss and sorrow in spending. Woe unto this sorrow-producing wealth!

❁　❁　❁

VII.241. He who has heard the declaration of *Shruti* "The knower of *Brahman* becomes *Brahman*", fixes his whole mind on *Brahman* and ultimately knows himself to be *Brahman*.

❁　❁　❁

VII.255. Let the ignorant people of the world perform worldly actions and desire to possess wives, children, and wealth. I am full of supreme bliss. For what purpose should I engage myself in worldly concerns?

❁　❁　❁

VII.260. Let those ignorant of the nature of *Brahman* listen to the teachings of Vedanta philosophy. I have Self-knowledge. Why again should I listen to them? Those who are in doubt reflect on the nature of *Brahman*. I have no doubts, so I do not do so.

❁　❁　❁

VII.272. An advocate of action is mainly concerned with the body, the organs of speech, the intellect and with *Karma*; he is not concerned with the witness - consciousness, whereas the illumined one is concerned with the associationless witness, not with other things.

ॐ

VII.291. As he has achieved all that was to be achieved, and nothing else remains for him to do, he feels satisfied and always thinks thus:

❖ ❖ ❖

VII.292. Blessed am I, blessed, for I have the constant vision of myself! Blessed am I, blessed, for the bliss of *Brahman* shines clearly to me!

❖ ❖ ❖

VII.295. Blessed am I, blessed, for there is nothing to compare with my great bliss! Blessed am I, blessed, blessed, blessed, again and again blessed!

❖ ❖ ❖

VIII.71. (For *kutastha*) there is no death, and no birth, none in bondage and none engaged in working out release (*sadhaka*), no aspirant nor release (*mumukshu*), and none liberated (*muktha*). That is the supreme Truth.

❖ ❖ ❖

IX.19. As the knowledge of *Sat-Chit-Ananda* has been acquired in the scriptural method, it, though an indirect knowledge, is not an illusory one.

❖ ❖ ❖

IX.43. The impediments of the present are (1) binding attachment to the object of the senses, (2) dullness of the intellect, (3) indulgence in improper and illogical arguments and (4) the deep conviction that the Self is an agent and an enjoyer.

❖ ❖ ❖

IX.118. The eternal Brahmanhood is revealed by knowledge and not created by it, for even in the absence of the revealer, the real entity does not cease to exist.

IX.121. It is better to perform the works ordained in the scriptures than be engrossed in worldly affairs. Better than this is to worship a personal deity and meditation on the attributeless *Brahman* is still better.

✿   ✿   ✿

IX.130. Those who give up meditation on the attributeless *Brahman* and undertake pilgrimages, recitations of the holy formulas, and other methods, may be compared to "those who drop the sweets and lick the hand".

✿   ✿   ✿

IX.155. Even if there is no realization, think "I am *Brahman*". Through meditation a man achieves even other things (like the Deities), why not *Brahman* who is ever-achieved?

✿   ✿   ✿

X.5. Bondage is caused by want of discrimination, and is negated by discrimination. Hence one should discriminate about the individual and Supreme Self.

✿   ✿   ✿

XI.34. In deep sleep the blind are not blind, the wounded not wounded, and the ill no longer ill, say the scriptures. All people too know this.

✿   ✿   ✿

XI.83. Do you simply say the word "*Brahman*" or do you see its meaning? If you know only the word, it remains for you to acquire knowledge of its meaning.

✿   ✿   ✿

XI.87. There are only three kinds of bliss experienced in the world: (1) *Brahmananda,* the bliss of *Brahman;* (2) *Vasanananda,* the bliss arising in the quiescent mind out of the impressions of *Brahmananda;* and (3) *Vishiayananda,* the bliss resulting from the fulfillment of the desire to be in contact with external objects.

❖ ❖ ❖

XII.53. When a tiger confronts men, it is hated; when it is away, it is disregarded; and when it has been tamed and made friendly, it causes joy; thus it is related to him and is loved.

❖ ❖ ❖

XII.55. The popular conclusion is that the Self is the dearest, the objects related to it are dear, and the rest are either disregarded or hated. This is also the verdict of Yajnavalkya.

❖ ❖ ❖

XII.60. A son is dearer than wealth, the body dearer than the son, the sense organs dearer than the body, life and mind dearer than the sense organs, and the Self is supremely dearer than life and mind.

❖ ❖ ❖

XII.68. Having considered all this, the disciple must abstain from forming an attachment to other things. He should focus his love on the Self and contemplate it day and night.

❖ ❖ ❖

XIII.6. The material cause is of three kinds: (1) the *Vivarta,* which gives rise to phenomenal appearance, not materially related to the cause; (2) the *Parinama,* which gives rise to an effect which is a modification or change of state of the cause; and (3) the *Arambha* which consists of effect being different from the causes. The last two (which presuppose parts) have no scope with reference to partless *Brahman.*

XIV.25. Thus Brihadratha described the defects pertaining to the body, the mind, and the objects of enjoyment: "As no one has liking for porridge vomited by a dog, likewise the man of discrimination also has no liking for the body etc."

❀   ❀   ❀

XV.31. In steady knowledge, existence, consciousness, and bliss shine as a single homogenous entity and not as separate entities, their difference having disappeared with the disappearance of their *Upadhi*-s (adjuncts).

Miscellaneous Gitas

Rama Gita
(Tattva-Sarayana)

IV.21. Bondage lies in the belief "I am the body". Liberation lies in the constant faith "I am *Brahman*". Hence an intelligent man should always meditate as "I am *Brahman*", by melting his ego in the Absolute.

❉ ❉ ❉

VII.14. When one is firmly rooted in Advaita, and when Dvaita is destroyed, then the world is perceived as a dream, due to one's being established in the highest state of Consciousness.

❉ ❉ ❉

XV.46. One who does not feel "this is good" and "that is not good", and eats whatever food he gets without attachment, who speaks the minimum, but truthfully, sweetly and appropriately, is really a man without tongue in the spiritual sense.

❉ ❉ ❉

XV.47. Whether casting a look on a baby born just now, or on a girl of sixteen, or on a woman one hundred years old, who is unperturbed, is really a eunuch.

❁   ❁   ❁

XV.48. Who walks only for the sake of *bhiksha* (alms) and for the sake of answering the calls of nature, who does not walk farther than a distance of eight or nine miles, is really a lame man.

❁   ❁   ❁

XV.49. Whose eyes do not look at anything, whether he is standing or walking, who does not look farther than four feet from his body, is really a blind *Bhikshu*.

❁   ❁   ❁

XV.50. Who is indifferent even after hearing good or bad, sweet or harsh words, which may cause sorrow or joy, is really deaf.

❁   ❁   ❁

XV.51. Even when objects of senses are rolling under his feet, and when he is capable of enjoyment, who remains like a man in deep sleep, with senses steadied, is called one devoid of consciousness.

❁   ❁   ❁

Rama Gita
(Adhyatma-Ramayana)

10. The performance of action does not destroy either ignorance or attachment. It leads to further pain of embodiment. Therefore, a wise man should abandon action, which is full of defects, and devote himself to knowledge and meditation.

ॐ

16. Therefore, let the wise man abandon all works. There can be no combination of knowledge with work, because work is opposed to knowledge. Let him withdraw the senses from all objects and devote himself always to the attainment of Self-Realization.

❖ ❖ ❖

Moksha Gita

3. Some indescribable Supreme principle, which is imperishable, unborn, undecaying, fearless, motionless, one without a second, ancient and infinite – that alone exists.

❖ ❖ ❖

7. *Brahman* cannot be defined. To define *Brahman* is to deny *Brahman*. The only adequate description of *Brahman* is a series of negatives. That is the reason why the *Uphanishad*-s declare: "*neti neti*" – "not this, not this".

❖ ❖ ❖

15. *Brahman* will not shine when the dualities of the mind are not destroyed. Destroy the dualities; *Brahman* will shine in its pristine glory.

❖ ❖ ❖

Uttara Gita

II.42. An ass laden with sandalwood knows only the weight on its back, and not the fragrance of it. Even so, one who studies many books, but knows not the Essence, carries merely the burden of booklore.

🕉

III.4. Life is fickle. Only the Imperishable Existence ("Be-ness") is to be known. Abandoning all scriptures and books, resort to what is Truth.

❁   ❁   ❁

III.7. To the Brahmins, God is in fire; to saints in the heart; to dull-headed men in idols; to equal-minded men everywhere.

❁   ❁   ❁

III.9. Wherever the mind goes, there and there it sees only the Supreme Truth. There and there, everywhere exists the Absolute *Brahman*.

❁   ❁   ❁

Jivanmukta Gita

5. He is called a *Jivanmukta* who, seeing the One *Brahman* existing in all beings, does not perceive any difference.

❁   ❁   ❁

15. He is called a *Jivanmukta* who partakes of the essence of the bliss of *Brahman*, and rejoices alone, and forever, being devoid of habits, natures, etc.

❁   ❁   ❁

Rishabha Gita

5. This loss of Self-awareness due to ignorance lasts as long as one does not enquire into the Truth of the Self; the mind lasts as long as there is action; the bondage of this mortal body is caused by action (*Karma*).

ॐ

18. He is not a *Guru*, he is not a relation, he is not a father, she is not a mother, it is not a Deity, he is not a Lord, who does not show the way of salvation to the *Jiva*.

❁   ❁   ❁

Shruti Gita

25. The *Shruti*-s said: Those who think that Being is born of Non-Being, or that the *Atman* dies, or that beings are many and different, or that rituals bear real fruits, teach to others their own misapprehensions. The notion of difference that *Purusha* is constituted of three *Guna*-s is due to ignorance of Thyself (the Supreme Lord); such difference is not in Thee; nor does that ignorance exist in Thee, for Thou art Absolute Consciousness.

❁   ❁   ❁

37. This universe did not exist in the beginning and it has no future existence; only the unreal universe in the middle is superimposed on Thee, who is the One Essence; therefore, it is compared to various forms of matter, viz., gold, nature, superimposition, etc.; this baseless fancy called the universe, the ignorant take as Real.

❁   ❁   ❁

Anu Gita

XXXV.30. Some dull-witted people praise *Karma*. The wise great-souled ones never praise *Karma*.

🕉

Shaunaka Gita

1. Shaunaka said: "Thousands of causes for grief and hundreds of causes for fear are there daily to an idiot." These do not exist for a wise man.

PART THREE

Ramana Wisdom

Teachings of Ramana Maharshi

Forgetfulness of your real nature is the real death, remembrance of it is the true birth. It puts an end to successive births. Yours is then eternal life.

❖ ❖ ❖

The relative happiness and unhappiness to the mind arise from sheer ignorance of the spiritual truth. Man's true nature is happiness, which is inborn. One's search for happiness is an unconscious search for the Self. At last, he finds what is already there. This happiness-bliss does not come to an end. It is eternal.

❖ ❖ ❖

What is the mind? If one searches to find out, then there would be no separate entity as the mind.

❖ ❖ ❖

The mind is a bundle of thoughts. They are dependent on the "I"-thought. Know the "I"-thought to be the mind.

❖ ❖ ❖

The mind is born of forms; rooted in forms. It feeds on forms, but is itself formless.

❖ ❖ ❖

Is there such a thing as the mind? If so what is its form? Does it have a beard or moustache?

❖ ❖ ❖

The "I"-thought is not really a thought like other thoughts. Because unlike the other *vritti*-s, which have no essential interrelation, the "I"-thought is equally and essentially related to each and every *vritti* of the mind. Without it there can be no other thoughts. It can subsist by itself without depending on the other thoughts. The "I"-thought is therefore fundamentally different from other thoughts. The search for its source is the search for the very source of "I am"-ness.

❖ ❖ ❖

What do you mean by complete realization? Does it mean becoming a stone, an inert mass? The *aham-vritti* is different from *aham-sphurti*. The former is the activity of the ego, and is bound to lose itself and make way for the latter which is an eternal expression of the Self. In Vedantic parlance this *aham-sphurti* is called *vritti-jnana*. Realization of *jnana* is always a *vritti*. There is a distinction between *vritti-jnana* or Realization and *Svarupa* the Real. *Svarupa* is *Jnana* itself, it is Consciousness. *Svarupa* is *Sat-Chit* which is omnipotent. It is always there self-attained. When you realize it, the realization is called *vritti-jnana*. It is only with reference to your existence that you talk of realization, of *jnana*. Therefore, when we talk of *jnana*, we always mean *vritti-jnana* and not *Svarupa-Jnana*; the *Svarupa* itself is *Jnana* (Consciousness) always.

❖ ❖ ❖

ॐ

No meditation on any kind of object is helpful. You must learn to realize that the subject and object are one. In meditating on an object whether concrete or abstract you are destroying the sense of oneness and creating duality. Meditate on what you are in reality... you will find...

❀ ❀ ❀

Here it is impossible for you to be without effort. When you go deeper, it is impossible for you to make any effort.

❀ ❀ ❀

The real *asana* is "being established" in the Self-Reality or the Source. Sit in your Self. Where can the Self go and sit? Everything sits in the Self. Find out the source of "I" and sit there. Do not have the idea that the Self cannot be realized without the help of *asana*-s, etc. They are not at all necessary. The chief thing is to enquire and reach the source of the ego. These details such as posture, etc., may distract the mind towards them or to the body.

❀ ❀ ❀

You may read whichever book you like. Self is the real book. You can look into it whenever you like. Nobody can take it away. It is always at hand to be read. Hold on to your Self in your spare time also, and then you can read any book.

❀ ❀ ❀

The wise regards the giving up of the notion "I am the body" as exhaling, self-enquiry as inhaling and abidance in the Heart as natural subsidence.

❀ ❀ ❀

Where is becoming? The thinker is all the while the same as the Real. He ultimately realizes that fact.

❀ ❀ ❀

Do not entertain such thoughts of imperfection, lack of qualities, etc. You are already perfect. Get rid of the ideas of imperfection and need for development. There is nothing to realize or annihilate. You are the Self. The ego does not exist. Pursue the enquiry and see if there is anything to be realized or annihilated. See if there is any mind to be controlled. Even the effort is being made by the mind which does not exist.

❖   ❖   ❖

You can only be the Self. To know the Self is to be it. Remain in the natural state.

❖   ❖   ❖

(Quoting the Bible he said) Be still and know that I am God (and added a rider), the Lord said "know" and not "think" that "I am God".

❖   ❖   ❖

In the eye of the *jnani* there are no others, so there is nothing like mingling with others for him.

❖   ❖   ❖

True surrender is the melting of the ego in its source, the heart. God is not deceived by outward acts. What he sees in the worshipper is how much of the ego remains in full control and how much is on the verge of destruction.

❖   ❖   ❖

When one surrenders, there will be no sense of doership in him. There will be a feeling of indifference and he will not be anxious about actions or their results. One will not commence any work for his own sake. Such a person would be the one who has renounced all action.

❖   ❖   ❖

We are familiar with a custom among some people in these parts based on deep sentiment of devotion to Lord *Ganesha*. Daily worship to his image, which is found installed in all the temples of the locality, is an indispensable ritual for these people before their daily meal. A certain poor traveler of this persuasion was passing through a sparsely inhabited country. Not finding a temple of *Ganesha* anywhere nearby where he could perform his daily worship to the image before his mid-day meal, he resolved to make an idol of the deity out of the small quantity of jaggery (brown sugar) he was carrying with him for his meal. Having made the idol out of jaggery, he proceeded earnestly with the ritual. However, when it came to the point in the ceremony where he had to make a small food offering to the deity, he discovered that he used all the jaggery he had to make the idol. But since no worship can be complete without the customary food offering, the simple-minded wayfarer pinched a small bit of jaggery from the idol itself and offered it to the deity. It did not occur to him that in the very act of pinching out a bit of jaggery he had defiled the very idol that he wanted to worship and made the offering worthless. Your idea of self-surrender is nothing better than the offering made by the wayfarer. By presuming your existence as something apart from the Supreme Being, you have merely defiled it. Whether you surrender yourself or not, you have never been apart from that Supreme Being. Indeed at this moment, even as in the past or the future, the divine alone is.

✿   ✿   ✿

Ego is non-existent, otherwise you would be two instead of one – you the ego, and you the Self. You are a single, indivisible whole. Enquire into yourself and the apparent ego and ignorance will disappear.

✿   ✿   ✿

ॐ

You are perfect, so abandon the idea of imperfection and need for development. Ego is not a real thing. It is the mind which makes the efforts and the mind is not real. Just as it is not necessary to kill the rope, which one imagines to be a snake, so also, there is no need to destroy the mind. Knowing the form of the mind makes the mind disappear.

❀ ❀ ❀

Our present world itself is not true. Each one sees a different imaginary world according to his imagination, and so where is the guarantee that the new world will be real? The individual, the world, and God, all of these are dependent on the True State. As long as there is the individual sense of "I", these are also there. From this individual sense of "I", from the mind, these three have arisen. If you destroy the mind, the three will not remain, but *Brahman* alone will remain, as it remains and abides even now. We see something incorrectly. This misperception will be rectified by enquiring into the real nature of this individual. Again after surrendering the mind, there will be nothing remaining but *Brahman*. Whether this world is real or unreal, consciousness or matter, a place of happiness or a place of misery, all these questions arise in the state of ignorance. They are not useful after Realization. The state of being fixed in the Self devoid of the individual feeling of "I" is the supreme state. In this state, there is no room for objective thinking, nor for this feeling of individual being. There is no doubt of any kind in this natural state of Being-Consciousness-Bliss.

❀ ❀ ❀

What can destiny do? It will not become operative if you make complete surrender. You will be free from worries. Mind becomes calm and peace will prevail.

❀ ❀ ❀

Every plane has its own illusion, which can be destroyed only by another illusion on the same plane. For example, a man takes a full meal and goes to sleep. He dreams of being hungry in spite of the food he ate while awake. To satisfy the dream hunger, he has to take dream food. A wound in a dream requires dream treatment. A great king once dreamt that he was ill but was too poor to call a doctor. He had to beg the doctor's fees from his friends to receive medical help. Although he had fabulous wealth in the waking state, it could be of no use to him in the dream state. Similarly the illusion of ignorance can be destroyed only by the illusion of the Master's teaching. Liberation is ever present and bondage absent, yet the universal experience is the reverse.

❀ ❀ ❀

Have you been born now? If really you have not been born now, then why think of the next birth? Truly, *karma* (action) does not trouble us, it is only the sense of doership that does. The idea of doing the karma or leaving it is false. Think who is the doer of *karma*.

❀ ❀ ❀

These are all intellectual concepts. No concept is realization. You must leave the intellect behind and be firm in intuition of the Self. None of these concepts are required even as aids for ensuring firmness, once perfect realization is attained. A man does not go on saying to himself, "I am a man, I am free, I am conscious", and so on. Realization is fullness of consciousness and is not complicated by thoughts like these.

❀ ❀ ❀

But the moment the ego-self tries to know itself, it changes its character, it begins to partake less and less of the *jada* in which it is absorbed, and more and more of the consciousness of the Self.

❀ ❀ ❀

ॐ

There is no teacher nor is there anyone to be taught, therefore there is no teaching.

✿   ✿   ✿

There is nothing nor is there anyone to become enlightened since the Self is already realized.

✿   ✿   ✿

The absolute is always with you, in you and you are yourself the absolute.

✿   ✿   ✿

Awareness, which already exists within everyone, everywhere, is imperishable and changeless.

✿   ✿   ✿

Your duty is to be and not to be this or that. The method is summarized in "Be still".

✿   ✿   ✿

The Bible says, "Be still and know that I am God." Stillness is the only requisite for the realization of the Self as God.

✿   ✿   ✿

Only silence is the eternal speech. The only words the heart to heart talk.

✿   ✿   ✿

Silence is truth. Silence is bliss. Silence is peace. And hence Silence is the Self.

✿   ✿   ✿

Consciousness is always Self-Consciousness. If you are consciousness of anything, you are essentially conscious of yourself.

❖ ❖ ❖

Unless you exist you cannot ask questions. So you must admit your own existence. That existence is the Self. It is already realized.

❖ ❖ ❖

Being what one already is, is effortless, since being is always present and always experienced.

❖ ❖ ❖

Even a learned man must bow before the illiterate sage. Illiteracy is ignorance; education is learned ignorance. Both of them are ignorant of their true aim; whereas a sage is not ignorant because there is no aim for him.

❖ ❖ ❖

The difficulty is that man thinks he is the doer. But it is a mistake. It is God who does everything and man is only a tool. If he accepts that position he is free from troubles, otherwise he courts them.

❖ ❖ ❖

There is not greater mystery than this – that, being the reality we seek to gain reality. We think that there is something hiding our reality and that it must be destroyed before the reality is gained. It is ridiculous. A day will dawn when you will yourself laugh at your past efforts. That which will be on the day you laugh is also here and now.

❖ ❖ ❖

ॐ

Realization is nothing to be gained afresh; it is already there. All that is necessary is to get rid of the thought "I have not realized".

❀   ❀   ❀

Realization is not acquisition of anything new nor is it a new faculty. It is only removal of all camouflage.

❀   ❀   ❀

The Self is always realized, it is not necessary to seek to realize what is already and already realized. For you cannot deny your own existence. That existence is consciousness, the Self.

❀   ❀   ❀

When you speak of a path, where are you now? And where do you want to go? If these are known, then we can talk of a path. Know first where you are and what you are. There is nothing to be reached. There is no goal to be reached. There is nothing to be attained. The conception that there is a goal and a path to it is wrong. We are the goal or peace always. You are the Self. You exist always.

❀   ❀   ❀

There is no reaching the Self. If Self were to be reached, it would mean that the Self is not here and now and that it is yet to be obtained. What is got afresh will also be lost. So it will be impermanent. What is not permanent is not worth striving for, so I say the Self is not reached. You are the Self, you are already that. You exist always. You are always as you really are. But you do not realize it. That is all.

❀   ❀   ❀

Always think what your real nature is; do not think of anything else.

❄   ❄   ❄

There is no alternative for you but to accept the world as unreal if you are seeking the Truth and the Truth alone.

❄   ❄   ❄

Self-enquiry is the direct path, all others are indirect paths. The first leads to the Self, the others elsewhere. Why waste time?

❄   ❄   ❄

Of all thoughts the thought "I" is the root, therefore the mind is only the thought "I".

❄   ❄   ❄

The Self is reached by the search for the origin of the ego and by diving into the heart.

❄   ❄   ❄

The Self is realized not by one's doing something, but by one's refraining from doing something, by remaining still and being simply what one really is.

❄   ❄   ❄

There is nothing like ignorance. It never arises. Everyone is of the nature of wisdom. The dispelling of ignorance is wisdom, which always exists.

❄   ❄   ❄

The mind is intangible, in fact it does not exist. The surest way to control it is to seek it. Then its activities cease.

❄   ❄   ❄

The mind cannot kill itself. So your business is to find the real nature of the mind. Then you will know that there is no mind. When the Self is sought, the mind is nowhere. Abiding in the Self, one need not worry about the mind.

❀   ❀   ❀

Self-enquiry alone can reveal the truth that neither the ego nor the mind really exist and enable one to realize the pure undifferentiated being of the Self or the absolute.

❀   ❀   ❀

Only the body has death and birth and it is illusion. There is in reality, neither birth nor death.

❀   ❀   ❀

There is really no reincarnation at all, either now or before. Nor will there be hereafter. This is the truth.

❀   ❀   ❀

Even the present is mere imagination, for the sense of time is purely mental. Space is similarly mental. Therefore, birth and rebirth, which take place in time and space, cannot be other than imagination.

❀   ❀   ❀

All that is necessary is to give up this mistaken identity, and that done, that ever-shining Self will be seen to be the single non-dual reality.

❀   ❀   ❀

We limit ourselves first, then seek to become the unlimited that we always are. All effort is only for giving up the notion that we are limited.

❀   ❀   ❀

This knowledge that there is nothing but God or Self, that "I" and "mine" do not exist and that only the Self exists, is *jnana*.

❈   ❈   ❈

Removal of the notion that we have not realized the Self is all that is required. We are always the Self. Only we do not realize it.

❈   ❈   ❈

The true state is the non-dual Self. It is eternal and abides whether one is aware or not.

❈   ❈   ❈

The body is a corpse. So long as one is in contact with it one must bathe in the waters of the Self.

❈   ❈   ❈

There is no creation in the state of Realization. When one sees the world, one does not see one's self. When one sees the Self the world is not seen. So see the Self and realize that there has been no creation.

❈   ❈   ❈

The dream water quenches dream thirst. The dream creation is however contradicted in the waking state. The waking creation is contradicted in other two states. What is not continuous cannot be real. What can be easier? The Self is more intimate than anything else. If that cannot be realized, is it easy to realize what is apart and farther away?

❈   ❈   ❈

Ignorance never arose. It has no real being. That which is, is only *vidya* (knowledge).

❈   ❈   ❈

To know the Self is to be the Self, as there are not two separate selves.

❖   ❖   ❖

If you are the body, why do they bury the corpse after death? The body must refuse to be buried.

❖   ❖   ❖

The ultimate truth is so simple. It is nothing more than being in the pristine state.

❖   ❖   ❖

Find out what is immediate, intimate, instead of trying to find out what is distant and unknown.

❖   ❖   ❖

Can anything be as direct as the Self – always experienced without the aid of the senses?

❖   ❖   ❖

Is there any way of adoring the Supreme, which is All, except by abiding firmly as That!

❖   ❖   ❖

All are in sleep, dreaming of the world and things and actions.

❖   ❖   ❖

Do not be that or this, but just be. Pure being is your nature.

❖   ❖   ❖

Be the Self; there will be no second thing to cause you fear.

❖   ❖   ❖

ॐ

Q: A Muslim visitor asked about *asana* (physical posture).
A: Abidance in God is the only true posture.

✿ ✿ ✿

The Self is always realized, look within and be still.

✿ ✿ ✿

You are always the Self and nothing but the Self.

✿ ✿ ✿

Existence and Consciousness is the only reality.
Consciousness plus waking, we call waking.
Consciousness plus sleep, we call sleep.
Consciousness plus dream, we call dream.

✿ ✿ ✿

Q: Does my realization help others?
A: Yes, certainly. It is the best help possible.
But there are no others to be helped.

✿ ✿ ✿

There is in reality no change, no creation.

✿ ✿ ✿

Do not meditate – be!
Do not think that you are – be!
Do not think about being – you are!

✿ ✿ ✿

Grace always Is and is not given.

✿ ✿ ✿

The ego-self does not exist at all.

✿   ✿   ✿

Be yourself and nothing more!

✿   ✿   ✿

To realize the Self is to be still.

✿   ✿   ✿

Liberation is our very nature.

✿   ✿   ✿

That which is, is Silence.

PART FOUR

Zen Wisdom

Teachings of Zen Masters

Lin-Chi

Those who are content to be nothing special are noble people. Don't strive. Be ordinary.

❀　❀　❀

Become a master of every situation, and you will always be in the right place.

❀　❀　❀

Someone asked, "What is the true nature of mind?"
The Master replied, "Officially even a needle cannot enter; unofficially you can drive a horse and cart through."

❀　❀　❀

Fellow believers, at this time, having found it impossible to refuse, I have been addressing you, putting forth a lot of trashy talk. But make no mistake! In my view, there are in fact no great numbers of principles to be grasped. If you want to use the thing, then use it. If you don't want to use it, then let it be.

❀　❀　❀

Someone asked, "What is the Buddha devil?"

The Master said, "If you have doubts in your mind for an instant, that's the Buddha devil. But if you can understand that the ten thousand phenomena were never born, that the mind is like a conjurer's trick, then not one speck of dust, not one phenomenon will exist. Everywhere will be clean and pure, and this will be Buddha. Buddha and devil just refer to two states, one stained, and one pure.

"As I see it, there's no Buddha, no living beings, no long ago, no now. If you want to get it, you've already got it – it's not something that requires time. There's no religious practice, no enlightenment, no getting anything, no missing out on anything. At no time is there any other *Dharma* than this. If anyone claims there is a *Dharma* superior to this, I say it must be a dream, a phantom. All I have to say to you is simply this.

❁   ❁   ❁

Followers of the Way, there are certain baldheads who turn all their efforts inward, seeking in this way to find some otherworldly truth. But they are completely mistaken! Seek the Buddha and you'll lose the Buddha. Seek the Way and you'll lose the Way. Seek the patriarchs and you'll lose the patriarchs.

❁   ❁   ❁

Followers of the Way, if you wish to be always in accord with the *Dharma*, never give way to doubt. "Spread it out and it fills the whole *Dharma*-realm, gather it up and it's thinner than a thread of hair." Its lone brightness gleaming forth, it has never lacked anything. "The eye doesn't see it, the ear doesn't hear it." What shall we call this thing? A man of old said, "Say something about a thing and already you're off the mark." You'll just have to see it for yourselves. What other way is there? But there's no end to this talk. Each of you, do your best! Thank you for your trouble.

❁   ❁   ❁

ॐ

If you want to be free, get to know your real Self. It has no form, no appearance, no root, no basis, no abode, but is lively and buoyant. It responds with versatile facility, but its function cannot be located. Therefore, when you look for it you become further from it, when you seek it you turn away from it all the more.

❀ ❀ ❀

Hui-Hai

After a considerable pause, they enquired, "How can *Mahaparinirvana* be attained?"
– By avoiding all samsaric deeds – those which keep you in the round of birth and death.
– What deeds are they?
– Well, seeking nirvana is a samsaric deed. Casting off impurity and clinging to purity is another. Harboring attainments and proofs of attainment is another, and so is failure to discard rules and precepts.
– Please tell us how to achieve deliverance.
– Never having been bound, you have no need to seek deliverance. Straightforward functioning and straightforward conduct cannot be surpassed.

❀ ❀ ❀

– How may we perceive our own nature?
– That which perceives is your own nature; without it, there could be no perception.

❀ ❀ ❀

ॐ

Your treasure house is within you. It holds all you ever need.

✿   ✿   ✿

– What method must we practice in order to attain deliverance?
– It can be attained only through a sudden illumination.
– What is a sudden illumination?
– "Sudden" means ridding yourselves of deluded thoughts instantaneously.
– "Illumination" means the realization that illumination is not something to be attained.

✿   ✿   ✿

– What shall I do to be awakened to it?
– It comes only by true intuition.
– What is it like?
– It resembles nothing.
– If so, it should be ultimately nonexistent.
– That which is nonexistent is not ultimate.
– Then it must exist.
– It does exist, but it is formless.

✿   ✿   ✿

Those who have perceived their own nature are no longer ordinary people. The Supreme Vehicle of sudden illumination transcends ordinary and holy alike. While deluded people are talking of ordinary and holy, illumined people leap over *Samsara* and *Nirvana* – both! While deluded people are speaking of facts and of the underlying principle, illumined people exercise their function without restriction. While deluded people seek achievement and realization, illumined people remain free from both. While deluded people set their hopes upon some far-distant eon, illumined people instantly perceive all.

✿   ✿   ✿

Hui-Neng

It is nonsense to insist that we cannot achieve enlightenment without learned and pious teachers. Because wisdom is innate, we can all enlighten ourselves.

❀   ❀   ❀

Understand the Abrupt Doctrine and external disciplines are unnecessary.

❀   ❀   ❀

The Truth is to be lived, not just mouthed.

❀   ❀   ❀

The secret is within your self.

❀   ❀   ❀

From the first not a thing is.

❀   ❀   ❀

Hsuen-Feng

We are like someone immersed in water, who complains of nothing to drink.

❀   ❀   ❀

Student: "What is the path to liberation?"
Seng-T'san: "Who binds you?"
Student: "No one binds me."
Seng-T'san: "Why then do you want to be liberated?"

❀   ❀   ❀

Sengai

I was born alone I will die alone. And between these two, I am
alone day and night.

❀   ❀   ❀

"All this Zen stuff is nonsense", said the skeptic.
"You are perfectly correct", responded the master,
"But this is a teaching I normally reserve only
for my most advanced students."

❀   ❀   ❀

Shen T'sing

This is the Great Mystery – you do and you don't exist.

❀   ❀   ❀

An enlightened being is its own light.
He can see in the dark.
He turns on the light only for his guests.
He uses ideas only to illuminate his visitors.

❀   ❀   ❀

Chiang Chin-Chi

For someone with a special gift or a certain sharpness of mind,
a gesture or a word is all that is needed to impart an immediate
perception of Truth.

❀   ❀   ❀

Dogen

When someone doesn't accept what you say, don't attempt to make him understand you intellectually. Don't enter into a debate. Listen to his objections until he begins to find his error himself.

❀ ❀ ❀

D.T. Suzuki

From the beginning nothing has been kept from you, all that you wished to see has been there all the time before you, it was only yourself that closed the eyes to the fact.

❀ ❀ ❀

Bodhidharma

If you use your mind to study reality, you will not understand either your mind or reality. If you study reality without using your mind, you will understand both.

❀ ❀ ❀

Daie

The teachings expounded in the Taoist, Confucian, and Buddhist scriptures are merely commentaries on the spontaneous cry – "Ah, This!"

❀ ❀ ❀

ॐ

I-Tuan

Speech is blasphemy; Silence is deception.
Beyond both is a way up, but my mouth is not wide enough to
point to it.

❀   ❀   ❀

Dosan

Wherever I go, there he is. He is no other than my self, but I
am not him.

❀   ❀   ❀

Ho-Shan

Just get rid of the false and you will automatically realize the
true.

❀   ❀   ❀

Seng-T'san

When you try to stop doing to achieve being, this very effort
fills you with doing.

❀   ❀   ❀

Yuan-Wu

There is only one Way – straight, open, and utterly empty of
obstructions.

❀   ❀   ❀

Lao Tau

To know that you do not know is the best.
To pretend to know when you do not know is a disease.

❖ ❖ ❖

Hashida

To study Buddhism is to study your own self.
To study your own self is to forget yourself.

❖ ❖ ❖

Huang-Po

Give up yourself to others.
Give up yourself to life.
Give up struggling to make sense of it all.
Simply, give up.

❖ ❖ ❖

Tao-Shan

Here It is, right now.
Start thinking about It and you miss It.

❖ ❖ ❖

ॐ

Ikkyu

I won't die.
I won't go anywhere.
Just don't ask me anything.

❁   ❁   ❁

Teaching of Kegon School

One embraces All.
All merges in One.
One is All.
All is One.
One pervades All.
All is in One.

❁   ❁   ❁

Zen Recitations

When the curious ask you what It is,
Don't affirm or deny anything.
Anything affirmed is not true,
Anything denied is not true.
How can someone say what It is,
When he hasn't fully known It?
And, knowing, what letters can be sent
From a land where words find no road to travel?
To their questions, therefore, offer silence.
Only silence and a pointing finger.

❁   ❁   ❁

ॐ

All things are empty,
They have no beginning and no end,
They are faultless and not faultless,
They are not perfect and not imperfect,
In this emptiness, there is no form,
No perception, no names,
No concepts, no knowledge,
There is no decay, nor death,
There are no Four Noble Truths,
No suffering, no origin of suffering,
No cessation of suffering,
And no path to the cessation of suffering,
There is no knowledge of *Nirvana*,
No obtaining it and no not obtaining it.

❖　❖　❖

Miscellaneous Zen Teachings

Ever since ancient times, many people have left their homes and loved ones to enter the gates of Buddhism and study Zen meditation. They spent a great amount of time and energy in discipline, contemplative training, but what is that they gain? If this question were posed to enlightened Zen masters, they would most likely answer: "Nothing."

When we stop differentiating, halt our delusions, and put an end to all thoughts, the two hindrances of discursive thought and intention will dissolve, and as our minds fill with peace, there will be "Nothing" we wouldn't understand.

❖　❖　❖

ॐ

There was once a wealthy man who asked the Zen monk, Sengai to create a work of calligraphy for him...

– "Father dies, son dies, grandson dies."
– Sengai, I wanted you to write something auspicious! What are you trying to pull?
– This is auspicious. If your sons were to die before you, or if your grandsons were to die before your sons, you would be extremely unhappy. If the people in your family live generation after generation and die according to this order, what is more auspicious than that?
– That makes sense.

❁   ❁   ❁

"Life is taxing, death is relaxing" (Zhuangzi). Death is like a weary traveler returning home. Isn't it the most fortunate thing for everyone to die in their natural order?

❁   ❁   ❁

One day, a nun named Wujincang asked the sixth Zen patriarch, Huneng:

– I have been studying the Nirvana Sutra for years and years, and there are still some passages that I don't quiet understand. Do you think you could explain them to me?
– I am sorry, but I can't read. If you can read the passages out for me, I will see if I can help you understand them.
– If you cannot even read the words, how can you understand the truth behind them?
– The truth and words are unrelated. The truth can be compared to the moon. And words can be compared to a finger. I can use my finger to point out the moon, but my finger is not the moon, and you don't need my finger to see the moon, do you?

Language is merely a tool for pointing out the truth, a means to help us attain enlightenment. To mistake words for the truth is almost as ridiculous as mistaking a finger for the moon.

❁   ❁   ❁

A young monk asked his teacher, Cishou:

– What do you call a person who feels something, but cannot put it into words?
– A mute person eating honey.
– And what do you call a person who doesn't feel anything, yet speaks with great vividness?
– A parrot calling someone.

In practicing Zen, we should be like the mute, gaining insights yet feeling it not worthwhile to discuss them with others. The worse thing a person can do is emulate a parrot and go around teaching others about one's merely superficial understanding of Zen.

❀   ❀   ❀

Xuanze asked the monk Qingfeng:

– What is the Buddha?
– The Fire God comes seeking fire.
– Ha, ha! I get it! I get it!
– I finally understand!
– What did you learn from Qingfeng?
– The Fire God is fire, yet he seeks fire from someone else. Just like, I am the Buddha, and yet I went to somebody else to ask about the Buddha.
– I thought you understood, but now I see you don't.
– What?! That had to be right! How can it be wrong?!
– Wait, wait… What is the Buddha?
– The Fire God comes seeking fire.
– Now I get it! Now I get it! This time I really understand!

Asking and answering are simply the rearranging of words; it is timing that is the most surprising of things! Xuanze could actually have attained enlightenment at any time.

❀   ❀   ❀

One day, the great General Kitagaki went to see his old pal, who was the Abbot of Tofuku Temple.

– The great general seeks an audience.
– I don't know any great generals.
– The master said he can't see you. He doesn't know any great generals.
– Oh, I'm sorry. Please go back and tell him it's Kitagaki that's here to see him.
– Okay, I'll give it a try.
– Ah, Kitagaki, please come in.

Name, position, achievements, and wealth often conceal the real Self inside, making one feel like a traveler who can't find his way home.

❀   ❀   ❀

There was once a farmer who discovered a priceless statute of one of the eighteen Buddhist Arhats (Holy men) on a hillside in a forest.

– That's gotta be a hundred pounds of pure gold!
– Ha, ha! We'll have enough to eat and drink forever!

The farmer's family and friends were all very excited about the find. But the farmer felt dejected and just sat around with a worried look on his face…

– You are a wealthy man now. What are you so worried about?
– Why, I still don't know where the other seventeen Arhats are!

Rich and pure are not functions of how much money we have, but rather, of whether or not we are content with what we have.

❀   ❀   ❀

There was once an old woman known as "Weeping Lady" because she cried all the time. On rainy days she would cry and on clear days she would cry...

– Old lady, why are you crying all the time?
– Because I have two daughters – one who married a shoe salesman and one who married an umbrella salesman. On days when the weather is good, I think of how my daughter's umbrella business is bad. And on rainy days, I think of how no one will go out to buy shoes from my other daughter!
– But on clear days, you should think of how good your daughter's shoe business is; and on rainy days, you should think of how good your other daughter's umbrella business is!
– Hey, you are right!

From that day on, the "Weeping Lady" wept no more. Instead, she chuckled to herself everyday regardless of the weather.

If "The mind is the Buddha", then whether a situation is good or bad, all depends on how you look at the situation.

✿   ✿   ✿

Once an official named Wei went to see the Zen master Xuansha.

– People say that we are always using it, but I still don't know what "It" is.
– Here, first have some melon seeds.
– Thank you!
– Uh, Master? You still haven't told me what "It" is.
– It's this! You have it everyday, and yet you don't know what "It" is!

Arriving at the Dao is not difficult. What's left is choosing it. Asking where the road lies is a great mistake because there is no road. We have been on the way (The Dao) all along.

❀   ❀   ❀

– What is the meaning of Zen?
– I would like to tell you…
– But right now I have to go and relieve myself.
– Think about it – such an insignificant affair, and yet I must do it for myself.
– Can you do it for me?

Coming to understand the big questions in life has to be done by one's self – no one else can do it for you. Maintaining other people's ideas is like the mimicry of a parrot – it may be speaking, but it doesn't know what it is saying.

❀   ❀   ❀

One day, the famous poet Bai Juyi asked the monk Niaowo about Zen:

– How must I lead my life so that I am completely at one with the Dao?
– Avoid all evil and perform all good.
– Even a three-year-old knows that much.
– A three-year-old may know it, but not even a one-hundred-year-old can do it.

❀   ❀   ❀

🕉

An old monk was drying vegetables under the scorching sun...

– How old are you?
– Sixty-eight.
– Why are you still working so hard here?
– Because I am here.
– But why are you working under the hot sun?
– Because the sun is there.

Heaven and earth nurture all things, but we should act without counting on the results and strive for success without dwelling on it. If we just work hard without complaining, we can become one with heaven and earth.

❀ ❀ ❀

– Two people were walking in the rain, and one person didn't get wet. Can any of you tell me why this is?
– Because one person was wearing rain gear.
– Because there were scattered showers, so one person didn't get rained on.
– Because one person was walking in the street and one person was walking under the eaves of buildings.
– You are all concentrating on the phrase "One person didn't get wet" so, of course, you'll never discover the reality.
– Look, if I say, "one person didn't get wet", Doesn't that mean they both got wet?

When a finger points at the moon, the moon is not on the finger; and when words point out the truth, the truth is not in the words. If we concentrate only on words, the words will stifle us, and we'll never see the truth.

❀ ❀ ❀

A monk asked Yueh-Shan: "What does one think of while sitting?"
The Master replied: "One thinks of not-thinking."
The monk asked: "How does one think of not-thinking?"
The Master said: "Without thinking."

❂   ❂   ❂

– What's that guy doing on the mountain over there?
– Let's go ask him.
– Are you standing here waiting for a friend?
– No.
– Then you are here to breathe the fresh air, right?
– No.
– Are you here to take in the beautiful scenery?
– No.
– Then why are you standing here?
– I am just here standing.

Most people live in a dualistic world of gains and losses, self and object. If the scenery is beautiful, I'm happy; if it's not, I'm disappointed.

❂   ❂   ❂

You cannot tread the Path before you have become that Path yourself.

❂   ❂   ❂

"Nothing but lies come out of my mouth", said the Master.
"There – see! I have just done it again."

❂   ❂   ❂

If you don't get It from yourself, where will you go for It?

❀ ❀ ❀

A heavy snowfall disappears into the sea. What silence!

❀ ❀ ❀

Two monks were arguing.
One said, "The flag is moving."
The other said, "No, the wind is moving."
On hearing their dispute, Hui-Neng said:
"It is neither the flag nor the wind that is moving.
It is your mind that moves."

❀ ❀ ❀

We have all, need nothing, are everything.
And all is One, just One, not two.

❀ ❀ ❀

Knock on the sky and listen to the sound!

❀ ❀ ❀

"When you seek It, you cannot find It."

❀ ❀ ❀

Student: "I am very discouraged.
What should I do?"
Soen Nakagwa: "Encourage others."

❁   ❁   ❁

Student: "I have nothing."
Master: "Then throw it away."

❁   ❁   ❁

Student: "What is Buddha?"
Yunmen: "Dried dung."

❁   ❁   ❁

Not this,
Not that,
Not anything!

೧೪೦

PART FIVE

Tao Wisdom

Teachings of Tao Masters

Chuang Tzu

The man in whom Tao acts without impediment harms no other being by his actions, yet he does not know himself to be "kind", to be "gentle"...
(He) does not bother with his own interests and does not despise others who do.
He does not struggle to make money and does not make a virtue of poverty.
He goes his way without relying on others and does not pride himself on walking alone. While he does not follow the crowd, he would not complain of those who do.
Rank and reward make no appeal to him; disgrace and shame do not deter him.
He is not always looking for right and wrong, always deciding "Yes" or "No".
The ancients said, therefore:

> "The man of Tao remains unknown.
> Perfect virtue produces nothing.
> 'No-self' is 'True-Self'.
> And the greatest man is nobody."

✿   ✿   ✿

One day, when Zhuangzi was fishing on the bank of the Pu River, two emissaries from Chu stopped by.

– Our King would like to hand over the affairs of our Government to you. Would you be willing?
– I have heard that there is a magical tortoise in Chu. It has been dead for three thousand years, but its shell was placed in a temple and is used for prognostication. You tell me, would that tortoise rather be dead with its shell held in high honor... or would it rather be alive and dragging its tail in the mud?
– Of course, it would rather be alive and dragging its tail in the mud!
– You guys can go back. I would rather drag my tail in the mud too.

To give up your original nature for the world's glory and power is a very serious case of confusion.

❁   ❁   ❁

Another day, Yen Huei again met Chungni (Confucius) and said:

"I am getting on."
"How so?"
"I can forget myself while sitting", replied Yen Huei.
"What do you mean by that?"
"I have freed myself from my body", answered Yen Huei. "I have discarded my reasoning powers. And by thus getting rid of my body and mind, I have become One with the Infinite. This is what I mean by forgetting myself while sitting."

❁   ❁   ❁

One day, the yellow emperor traveled north of the Chi River and ascended a slope of the Kunlun Mountains. On his way back, he lost his mysterious pearl...

🕉

He ordered "Knowledge" to go look for it, but he couldn't find it.

Then he sent Li Zhu to look for it with his keen eyes, but he couldn't find it.

Chi Gou, the great debater, searched, but he couldn't find it either.

– "Formless", why don't you go look for it?

– Yes, your majesty.

Finally it was "Formless" who found the mysterious pearl.

How strange that only "Formless" was able to find the pearl!

The Dao cannot be obtained by way of knowledge, the senses, or debate. Only non-intention and non-affectation can find it – because the Dao is a realm beyond the intellect and the senses.

❀ ❀ ❀

Dongguozi asked Zhuangzi:

– That Dao you're always talking about – where is it?

– It's everywhere.

– Can you point it out, please?

– The Dao is in this ant.

– Such a lowly thing.

– The Dao is those weeds.

– Even more lowly.

– The Dao is in a clay tile.

– You keep going further down.

– The Dao is in defecation.

– Hee, Hee! What's the matter?

– Your questions were far from the Dao. In observing the myriad things with the Dao in mind, there is no high or low status. Ants, weeds, clay tiles, and defecation are all the same. If they weren't in accord with the Dao, they wouldn't exist. That's why I say the Dao is everywhere.

❀ ❀ ❀

🕉

When Zhuangzi's wife died, Huizi went to pay his respects. When he arrived, he saw Zhuangzi crouched down drumming and singing.

– All these years your wife takes care of the house and kids, then she gets old and dies, and not only you don't cry, but you drum and sing! That's outrageous!
– Not really. When she had just passed away, how could I not have felt anything? But then I thought for a bit: originally people don't have life, or even a body or spirit... Then somewhere in the vague and indiscernible, there's a change, and a spirit issues forth, then another change and there is a body, and another change and there is life. Now there has been another change and my wife has passed away. It's as natural as a passing of the four seasons. She is already resting peacefully in the giant chamber of nature. So if I start bawling about it, it would seem that I don't understand the fate of things.

The meaning of life lies in confirming to the natural processes. When you are a child, be a child. When you are an adult, be an adult; when you are old, be old. Live when it's time and die when it's time.

❖   ❖   ❖

Taiqing asked "Inexhaustible":

– Do you know the Dao?
– No.

Taiqing then asked "Non-action":

– Do you know the Dao?
– Sure.
– Can it be described?
– Yes. You can call it prestigious and lowly. You can say that it coalesces and disperses.
– I still don't understand. I will ask "Beginingless".

– "Inexhaustible" didn't know, but "Non-action" did. What do you think?

– The one who knows is shallow, and the one who doesn't is profound!

– Oh, so the Dao can't be heard with the ears, seen with the eyes, or spoken with the mouth, the Dao is beyond sensory knowledge.

The Dao cannot be asked about; If it is asked about, there is no answer. To force a question when it can't be asked is to ask a hollow question. To force an answer when there is no answer is meaningless.

✿   ✿   ✿

Shun once asked Cheng:

– Can the Dao be possessed?

– You don't even possess your own body. How could you possess the Dao?

– If my body doesn't belong to me, who does it belong to?

– Your body, your life, your children and grandchildren are all temporary gifts from nature. How can you say they are yours?

For a person of the Dao, to ignorantly believe that he owns his body is a kind of confusion. To intentionally try to possess the Dao is also confusion.

✿   ✿   ✿

– All my life I have said so many things, but...

– I have never really said a single word.

We are always debating one thing or another, but does what we say really mean anything? Maybe it would be better to say nothing and continue merrily on our way.

✿   ✿   ✿

Once there was a man who hated his own shadow. When he walked and found that his shadow was close behind him, he began to walk faster and faster. But the faster he moved, the closer his shadow came. So he ran like a madman, and in the end, he dropped dead.

Those who do not understand the Tao are just like the man who hated his shadow. It is actually very easy to be rid of one's shadow – just rest under a tree. Just rest!

❁　❁　❁

To exercise no-thought and rest in nothing is the first step toward resting in Tao. To start from nowhere and follow no road is the first step toward attaining Tao.

❁　❁　❁

Great knowledge sees all in One. Small knowledge breaks down into the many.

❁　❁　❁

All the fish needs is to get lost in the water.
All the man needs is to get lost in Tao.

❁　❁　❁

Minds free, thoughts gone.
Brows clear, faces serene.

❁　❁　❁

Chang Tzu

Be content with the moment and willing to follow the flow.

❁　❁　❁

Embrace all beings, for all are One.

❁　❁　❁

All theories are completely false.

❁　❁　❁

🕉

Lao Tzu

Once Zhuang Zhou dreamed he was a butterfly, a fluttering butterfly. What fun he had, doing as he pleased! He did not know he was Zhou. Suddenly he woke up and found himself to be Zhou. He did not know whether Zhou had dreamed he was a butterfly or a butterfly had dreamed he was Zhou. Between Zhou and the butterfly there must be some distinction. This is what is meant by the transformation of things.

❀ ❀ ❀

True words are not pleasant to hear; words that are pleasant to hear are not true. A good person doesn't argue; an argumentative person is not good. A wise person understands that the great Tao of the Universe lies within one's own heart and that it isn't necessary to run around in search of it.

❀ ❀ ❀

Those who prattle on and on understand nothing about Tao. Don't reveal your sharpness; eliminate all complications; withhold your brightness; merge with the dusty world. This is the realm of mysterious identity.

❀ ❀ ❀

When pursuing knowledge, you will experience a daily increase. But, when pursuing the Dao, you will experience a daily decrease – less and less every day, until you arrive at the realm of non-action.

❀ ❀ ❀

Understanding the good and the bad in other people is merely intelligence, while understanding one's own nature is true enlightenment.

✿ ✿ ✿

We shape clay into a pot, but it is the emptiness inside that holds whatever we want.

✿ ✿ ✿

Nothing is better than the wordless teaching and the advantage of non-action.

✿ ✿ ✿

If you think you can speak about the Tao, it is clear you don't know what you're talking about.

✿ ✿ ✿

Be at peace. Be aware of the Source. This is the fulfillment of your destiny. Know that which never changes. This is enlightenment.

✿ ✿ ✿

Trying to understand is like trying to see through muddy water. Be still and allow the mud to settle.

✿ ✿ ✿

The acceptable and the unacceptable are both acceptable.

✿ ✿ ✿

The wise succeeds without intending to do so.

✿ ✿ ✿

Something mysteriously formed,
Born before heaven and earth.
In the silence and the void,
Standing alone and unchanging,
Ever present and in motion.
Perhaps it is the mother of ten thousand things.
I do not know its name.
Call it Tao.

❀ ❀ ❀

Hua Ching Ni

Tao is the pointing finger and, at the same time, the direction.

❀ ❀ ❀

Lieh Tzu

A Taoist laughs at social conventions, and eludes or adapts himself to them.

❀ ❀ ❀

Hua Hu Ching

To manage your mind, know that there is nothing, and then relinquish all attachment to nothingness.

❀ ❀ ❀

Because clarity and enlightenment are within your own nature, they are regained without moving an inch.

❀   ❀   ❀

Remember: if you can cease all restless activity, your integral nature will appear.

❀   ❀   ❀

Li Po

We sit together, the Mountain and I, till... only the Mountain remains.

❀   ❀   ❀

The great way is very smooth; but the people love the bypath.

❀   ❀   ❀

Confucius

In antiquity men studied for their own sake, nowadays men study for the sake of (impressing) others.

OM SHANTI SHANTI SHANTI !

Appendixes

The Four Mathas Established by Shri Adi Shankara

Matha	Jyoti (Badrinath)	Shringeri (Sringeri)	Govardhana (Puri)	Sharada (Dvaraka)
Sannyasa Dasanami	Giri Sagara Parvata	Puri Bharati Sarasvati	Vana Aranya	Tirtha Ashrama
Brahmacharya	Nanda/Ananda	Chaitanya	Prakasha	Svarupa
Veda	Atharva	Yajur	Rig	Sama
Devata	Narayana	Adi Varaha	Jagannatha	Siddheshvara
Devi	Purnagiri	Kamakshi	Vrishala	Bhadrakali
Kshetra	Badarikashrama	Rameshvara	Puri	Dvaraka
Acharya	Totaka	Sureshvara	Hastamalaka	Padmapada
Sampradaya	Anandavara: Freedom from desire for sensual pleasures	Bhurivara: Freedom from desire for worldly treasures	Bhogavara: Freedom from desire for enjoyment	Kitavara: Freedom from tendencies hurtful to creatures
Tirtha	Alakananda	Tungabhadra	Mahodadhi	Gomati
Mahavakya	Ayam Atma Brahma	Aham Brahmasmi	Prajnanam Brahma	Tat Tvam Asi
Gotra	Bhrigu	Bhurbhuvah	Kasyapa/Avya	Agni
Svadhyaya	Giri (Mundaka) Parvata (Prasna) Sagara (Mandukya)	Puri (Katha) Bharati (Taittiriya) Sarasvati (Brihadaranyaka)	Vana (Aitareya) Aranya (Kaushitaki)	Tirtha (Kena) Ashrama (Chandogya)

Dasanami and Their Meaning

(Ten Suffixes Added to the Sannyasa Names)

(1)	*TIRTHA* : The one who always take bath in the holly union of the three rivers, namely "*Tat Tvam Asi* ", with the whole mind concentrated on the meaning of "*Tat Tvam Asi*" is called "*Tirtha*".
(2)	*ASHRAMA* : The one who has taken *sannyasa* with full maturity, the one who is free from bondage of desire, the one who does not come and go anywhere is called "*Ashrama*".
(3)	*VANA* : The one who lives in a jungle or forest in a lonely but beautifully place freed from all desires is called "*Vana*".
(4)	*ARANYA* : The one who is always established in a jungle, forest, garden or a vacant piece of land, renouncing the entire world is called "*Aranya*".
(5)	*GIRI* : The one who always stays in a mountain engaged in the study of *Gita*, profound, with a firm and unshaken intellect is called "*Giri*".
(6)	*PARVATA* : The one who lives beneath mountains, has a profound knowledge and knows that which is the Essence is called "*Parvata*".
(7)	*SAGARA* : The one who is deep in the ocean of the final truth, the one who possesses gems of knowledge and the one who never transgresses the limits of law and discipline is called "*Sagara*".
(8)	*SARASVATI* : The one who is always engaged in the knowledge of musical notes, a good musician and a good poet and the one who annihilates the bad taste of the ocean of this phenomenal world is called "*Sarasvati*".
(9)	*BHARATI* : The one who has left all the other burdens but is full of knowledge and the one who does not know the burden of sorrow is called "*Bharati*".
(10)	*PURI* : The one who is full of the ultimate knowledge of the self and who is established fully in the ultimate truth and who is engaged in the contemplation of the supreme *Brahman* is called "*Puri*".

Tenets of Advaita and Vishishtadvaita Vedanta

Tenets of Advaita (non-dualism) School of Shankara		Tenets of Vishishtadvaita (qualified non-dualism) School of Ramanuja
Reality is one alone, it is *Brahman*, and there is nothing else.	(1)	Reality is *Narayana*, who is qualified by His body (the world), which consists of matter and soul.
Anything at all other than *Brahman* is not real; whether it belongs to the same class as *Brahman*, to a different class from *Brahman* or is located in *Brahman*. *Brahman* is indeed bereft of the threefold difference, having something belonging to the same class or something belonging to a different class.	(2)	*Narayana* is different from the individual souls who belong to the same class as Himself on account of being sentient. *Narayana* is different from the inert primary matter, which belongs to a different class on account of being insentient, and *Narayana* is different from the qualities which produce what is auspicious and which belong to Himself.
Brahman is free from characteristics. It cannot be said in any way that it is "such and such".	(3)	*Narayana* possesses characteristics. Endowed with such characteristics as omniscience, eternity, pervasiveness etc. it can be expressed by words such as "all knowing", "eternal", "all pervasive", etc.
For this very reason, *Brahman* is free from qualities. Even those qualities which produce what is auspicious do not exist in *Brahman*.	(4)	*Narayana* is by nature the locus of numerous groups of qualities, which produce what is auspicious, such as the nature of being free from sin and so forth. Qualities which should be abandoned do not exist in *Narayana*.

ॐ

Tenets of Advaita (non-dualism) School of Shankara		Tenets of Vishishtadvaita (qualified non-dualism) School of Ramanuja
A quality, even in the form of consciousness, does not exist in *Brahman*. But consciousness is the essential nature of *Brahman*.	(5)	Even though *Narayana* is of the nature of consciousness, it is the locus of consciousness, which is a quality. But the consciousness, which is a quality, is certainly different from the consciousness which is the essential nature of *Narayana*.
For this reason, in reality knowership does not exist in *Brahman*. But the expression "He is a knower" is of a figurative nature.	(6)	Therefore the knowership on the part of *Narayana* is certainly a reality. And for this reason the expression "He is a knower" is true.
Brahman is not even an object of knowledge. Because it is impossible for Itself to be the consciousness and the object of consciousness.	(7)	*Narayana* is certainly an object of knowledge as well. Because the consciousness is a quality and different from *Narayana*, therefore it is possible for *Narayana* to be the locus of consciousness, which is a quality, and the object of consciousness.
Brahman is both being and consciousness. But consciousness does not have being as its object.	(8)	*Narayana* is being, and the consciousness, which is a quality, is not the being, but has being as its object.
Brahman is eternally unchangeable in Its own nature. And in that very nature It is without a second.	(9)	*Narayana* is eternally unchangeable in His own nature. But He is subject to transformation, in the manner of being qualified by a body consisting of what is sentient and insentient.
For this reason, it is said: "*Brahman* is non-dual (*advaya*)."	(10)	The non-duality of *Narayana* is not the non-duality of the modes (individual souls and insentient objects) but the non-duality of the possessor of the modes, who is one alone.

🕉

Tenets of Advaita (non-dualism) School of Shankara		Tenets of Vishishtadvaita (qualified non-dualism) School of Ramanuja
Brahman alone appears as *Ishvara*, the Lord, who has *maya* as his limiting adjunct and *Brahman* alone is *jiva*, the individual soul, who has *avidya* as his limiting adjunct. What is insentient exists only in appearance and is certainly unreal. Thus reality is one alone.	(11)	*Narayana* is the Lord, and the class of individual souls and the class of insentient objects, which constitute His body, are certainly different from Him. Thus reality is threefold, consisting of what is sentient, what is insentient and *Narayana*, the Lord.
The power of *Brahman* has three qualities and although it is non-different from *Brahman* it is as though different. It can be expressed by the words *ajnana* etc. *Brahman*, as conditioned by that power, is the primary material cause of the world.	(12)	The primary matter consists of three qualities, it is in reality different from *Narayana* and it is the primary material cause of the world.
The world appears in *Brahman* alone due to ignorance. This is the doctrine of false appearance (*vivarta-vada*).	(13)	The primary matter alone transforms into the form of the world on account of the presence of the Lord who is the inner controller. This is the doctrine of real transformation (*parinama-vada*).
This world, which exists only in appearance, being a false appearance of *Brahman*, is certainly unreal. This is, the absolute truth (*paramarthika-satya*).	(14)	This world, which is a real transformation of the primary matter, is certainly real.
This world, which is indeterminable (as absolutely real or absolutely unreal), appears due to the error called "ignorance". Therefore there is the apprehension of what is indeterminable. This is the illusory truth (*pratibhasika-satya*).	(15)	In reality, the world is recognized as only real. Therefore in all places there is the apprehension of the real.
In the case of silver on a pearl-oyster and in dream, etc., the objects perceived are indeed indeterminable as real or unreal.	(16)	In the case of silver on a pearl-oyster and in dream, etc. the objects perceived are certainly real.

Tenets of Advaita (non-dualism) School of Shankara		Tenets of Vishishtadvaita (qualified non-dualism) School of Ramanuja
The scripture too is unreal because it is included within the world. Still it is certainly the means for the knowledge of reality, like a useful object in a dream.	(17)	Because the scripture is certainly real it is the means for the knowledge of reality. Because the origination of the real from the unreal is not possible.
The means of knowledge (pramana-s) are six: perception, inference, verbal testimony, comparison, indirect inference and non-apprehension.	(18)	The means of knowledge (pramana-s) are three: perception, inference and verbal testimony.
When knowledge arises through the means of knowledge, the internal-organ manifests the knowledge in the internal-organ.	(19)	The knowledge, which arises through the means of knowledge, is in reality located in the individual soul.
The "I-entity", which appears as the locus of consciousness, is not the individual soul. But the "I-entity" is the "I-notion", which is a mode of the internal organ.	(20)	The "I-entity", which is the locus of consciousness, is certainly the individual soul. Whereas the "I-notion", which is different from the "I-entity", is not the locus of consciousness.
The individual soul is pervasive.	(21)	The individual soul is minute.
The individual soul, by its very nature pervades all the limbs of the body.	(22)	The individual soul pervades all the limbs of the body by means of consciousness.
The individual soul has only Brahman as its essential nature and is thus one alone. Whereas the apparent multiplicity of souls pertains to the limiting adjuncts.	(23)	The individual soul is, in reality, manifold. Whereas the non-duality of souls is the non-duality of the possessor of the modes.
The commencement of the inquiry into Brahman follows the accomplishment of the fourfold means.	(24)	The commencement of the inquiry into Narayana follows the knowledge of the nature of rituals.
Even verbal testimony produces perceptual knowledge in the presence of all the requirements for perception.	(25)	The knowledge arising from verbal testimony is only mediate; it is never perceptual.

Tenets of Advaita (non-dualism) School of Shankara		Tenets of Vishishtadvaita (qualified non-dualism) School of Ramanuja
The cessation of ignorance follows immediately upon the direct apprehension of the essential nature of *Brahman* produced by the *mahavakya*-s, etc.	(26)	*Narayana* is pleased by the intense devotional meditation produced by the *mahavakya*-s, etc.
Upon the apprehension of *Brahman*, who is beyond happiness and sadness, there is liberation while alive (*jivan-mukti*), even though the physical body continues to exist.	(27)	There is no liberation while alive (*jivan-mukti*). Because the experience of happiness and sadness is inevitable if the physical body continues to exist.
When there is the relinquishment of the physical body upon the destruction of the karma, which had begun to operate, one abides in *Brahman*, one's own essential nature.	(28)	When there is the relinquishment of the physical body upon the destruction of the karma, there is similarity with *Narayana* due to acquisition of a divine body.
This is the liberation after the death of the physical body (*videha-mukti*), but the only true liberation is liberation while alive (*jivan-mukti*).	(29)	This is liberation after the death of body and it is the only true liberation.
There is no "I-ness" in the state of liberation while alive (*jivan-mukti*).	(30)	"I-ness" exists even in the state of liberation after death.
In Liberation there is absolutely no difference between the individual soul and *Brahman*, the Absolute. What remains is *Brahman* alone.	(31)	The difference between the individual soul and *Narayana*, the Lord, certainly exists even in Liberation.
In this supreme state is no trace of sorrow, nor is there any trace of happiness.	(32)	In this supreme state is experienced an abundance of pleasure, which is completely devoid of any trace of sorrow.

Tenets of
Vivarana and Bhamati
Schools

Vivarana - Prasthana		Bhamati - Prasthana
(a) *Brahman* is the locus of cosmic *avidya* (*maya*). (b) *Jiva* is the locus of individual *avidya*.	(1)	*Jiva* is the locus of both cosmic *avidya* (*maya*) and individual *avidya*. *Brahman*, being of the nature of *vidya* (knowledge), cannot be the locus of *avidya* (ignorance).
(a) Cosmic *avidya* (*maya*) is one. (b) Individual *avidya* is manifold.	(2)	*Avidya* is different in each *jiva* and is therefore manifold.
Avidya has as its object *Brahman*.	(3)	*Avidya* has as its object *Brahman*.
Avidya possesses a twofold power: (a) Veiling power (*avarana-shakti*), (b) Projecting power (*vikshepa-shakti*).	(4)	*Avidya* possesses only the veiling power (*avarana-shakti*).
Avidya is the efficient (*nimitta*) cause of the world in the capacity of being an error and is also the material (*upadana*) cause.	(5)	*Avidya* is the efficient (*nimitta*) cause in the capacity of being an error.
Brahman and *maya* are the material (*upadana*) cause of the world: (a) *Brahman* is the illusory or apparent cause (*vivartopadana*), (b) *Maya* is the real or transforming material cause.	(6)	*Brahman* alone is the material cause of the world as illusory or apparent cause (*vivartopadana*).
Shravana (hearing) is the main factor in Realization, while *manana* (reflection) and *nididhyasana* (deep meditation) are auxiliaries.	(7)	*Nididhyasana* (deep meditation) is the main factor in Realization, while *shravana* (hearing) and *manana* (reflection) are auxiliaries.

ॐ

Vivarana - Prasthana		Bhamati - Prasthana
Pure *Brahman* and the associated *Brahman* are the objects of Vedantic knowledge.	(8)	Only the associated *Brahman* is the object of Vedantic knowledge and not pure *Brahman*.
Pure Consciousness is neither the object of mental modification (*vritti*) nor of the reflected consciousness.	(9)	Pure Consciousness is the object of mental modification (*vritti*).
Knowledge is a mental action, but does not come under the scope of Vedic injunctions.	(10)	Knowledge is not a mental action and does not come under the jurisdiction of Vedic injunctions.
There is no injunction in the act of study (*shravana*) of the Upanishadic texts.	(11)	There is no injunction in the act of study (*shravana*) of the Upanishadic texts.
The sense organs, superimposed as they are on the witnessing self (*sakshin*), are perceptible.	(12)	Only the characteristics of the sense organs are imposed on the witnessing self (*sakshin*) and as such are perceptible.
Jiva-s are *pratibimba*-s, or reflections of *Brahman* in *antahkarana* (internal organ). The reflected images have no reality other than that of the original *bimba* (*Brahman*). This doctrine is called *pratibimba-vada* (the doctrine of reflection).	(13)	*Jiva*-s are appearances of *Brahman* being limited by *avidya*. Just as a pot limits infinite space, individual *avidya* limits *Brahman* and makes it appear as *jiva*-s. This doctrine is called *avaccheda-vada* (the doctrine of limitation).
Moksha is attained simultaneously with *jnana* and the continuance of the body does not impose any limitation. Hence, only *jivan-mukti* (liberation while alive) is recognized as true Liberation.	(14)	*Moksha* is not attained simultaneously with *jnana*, for the continuance of the body imposes limitation, implying the existence of a trace of *avidya*. Only the death of the body puts an end to this trace of *avidya* and confers liberation. Hence, only *videha-mukti* (liberation after death) is admitted as true Liberation.

ॐ

Classification of Advaitic Analogies

I.	Explanatory analogies	II.	Effective analogies
1)	Causal analogies	1)	Popular analogies
a)	Creation analogies		
	- *lodestone*		- *fire / sparks*
	- *hypnotist, gods, king*		- *boat / shore*
	- *dream*		- *worm / wasp*
b)	Transformation analogies		- *female crane*
	- *actor*		- *lotus*
	- *thread / cloth*		- *sympathy*
	- *clay / pot*		- *carpenter*
	- *ocean / waves*		- *eclipse*
c)	Realization analogies		
	- *tenth man*		
	- *lost necklace*		
	- *loss of direction*		
	- *soap-nut*		
2)	Structural analogies	2)	Scriptural analogies
a)	Brahman / World analogies		
	- *mirage*		- *spider*
	- *sky surface*		- *lump of salt*
	- *firebrand*		- *clay / pot*
	- *rope / snake*		- *milk / curd*
	- *post / man*		- *water / ice*
	- *shell / silver*		- *gold / ornament*
b)	Atman / Jiva analogies		
	- *double moon*		
	- *crystal / color*		
	- *light / object*		
	- *object / mirror image*		
	- *space / pot-space*		

Classification of Hindu Scriptures

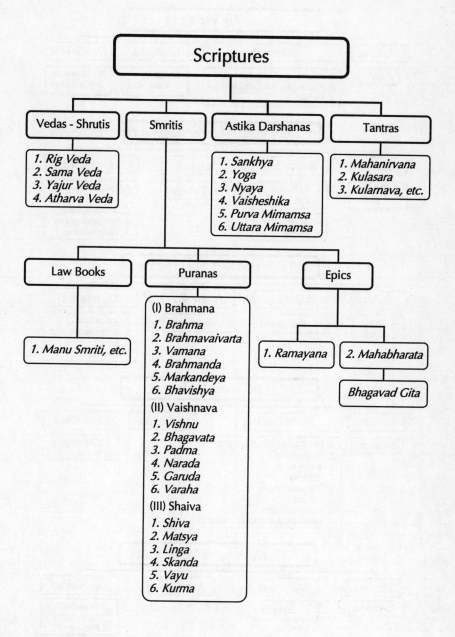

Scriptures

Vedas - Shrutis
1. Rig Veda
2. Sama Veda
3. Yajur Veda
4. Atharva Veda

Smritis

Astika Darshanas
1. Sankhya
2. Yoga
3. Nyaya
4. Vaisheshika
5. Purva Mimamsa
6. Uttara Mimamsa

Tantras
1. Mahanirvana
2. Kulasara
3. Kularnava, etc.

Law Books
1. Manu Smriti, etc.

Puranas

(I) Brahmana
1. Brahma
2. Brahmavaivarta
3. Vamana
4. Brahmanda
5. Markandeya
6. Bhavishya

(II) Vaishnava
1. Vishnu
2. Bhagavata
3. Padma
4. Narada
5. Garuda
6. Varaha

(III) Shaiva
1. Shiva
2. Matsya
3. Linga
4. Skanda
5. Vayu
6. Kurma

Epics
1. Ramayana
2. Mahabharata

Bhagavad Gita

The Four Sections of Vedas

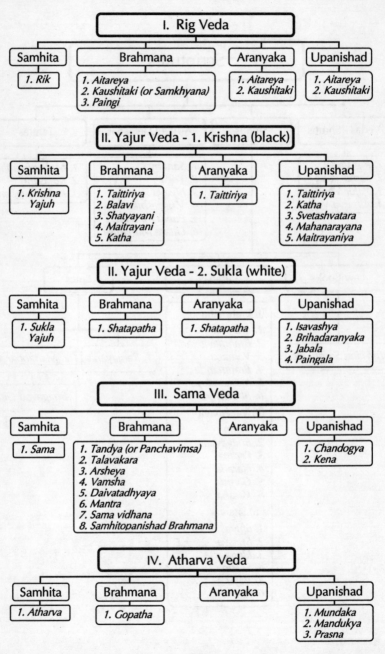

I. Rig Veda

Samhita	Brahmana	Aranyaka	Upanishad
1. Rik	1. Aitareya 2. Kaushitaki (or Samkhyana) 3. Paingi	1. Aitareya 2. Kaushitaki	1. Aitareya 2. Kaushitaki

II. Yajur Veda - 1. Krishna (black)

Samhita	Brahmana	Aranyaka	Upanishad
1. Krishna Yajuh	1. Taittiriya 2. Balavi 3. Shatyayani 4. Maitrayani 5. Katha	1. Taittiriya	1. Taittiriya 2. Katha 3. Svetashvatara 4. Mahanarayana 5. Maitrayaniya

II. Yajur Veda - 2. Sukla (white)

Samhita	Brahmana	Aranyaka	Upanishad
1. Sukla Yajuh	1. Shatapatha	1. Shatapatha	1. Isavashya 2. Brihadaranyaka 3. Jabala 4. Paingala

III. Sama Veda

Samhita	Brahmana	Aranyaka	Upanishad
1. Sama	1. Tandya (or Panchavimsa) 2. Talavakara 3. Arsheya 4. Vamsha 5. Daivatadhyaya 6. Mantra 7. Sama vidhana 8. Samhitopanishad Brahmana		1. Chandogya 2. Kena

IV. Atharva Veda

Samhita	Brahmana	Aranyaka	Upanishad
1. Atharva	1. Gopatha		1. Mundaka 2. Mandukya 3. Prasna

Brahman and Jiva

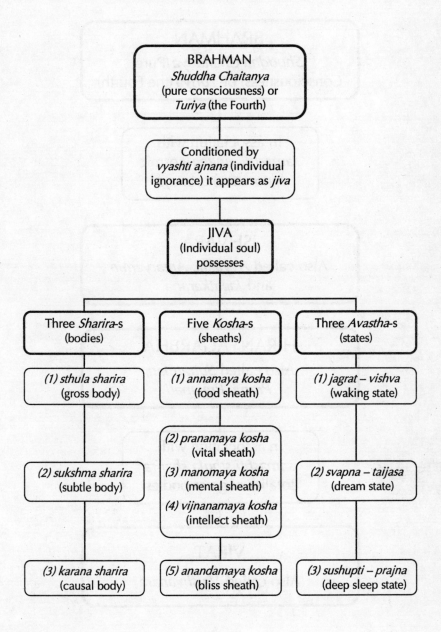

BRAHMAN
Shuddha Chaitanya
(pure consciousness) or
Turiya (the Fourth)

Conditioned by
vyashti ajnana (individual
ignorance) it appears as *jiva*

JIVA
(Individual soul)
possesses

Three *Sharira*-s
(bodies)

Five *Kosha*-s
(sheaths)

Three *Avastha*-s
(states)

(1) sthula sharira
(gross body)

(1) annamaya kosha
(food sheath)

(1) jagrat – vishva
(waking state)

(2) pranamaya kosha
(vital sheath)

(2) sukshma sharira
(subtle body)

(3) manomaya kosha
(mental sheath)

(2) svapna – taijasa
(dream state)

(4) vijnanamaya kosha
(intellect sheath)

(3) karana sharira
(causal body)

(5) anandamaya kosha
(bliss sheath)

(3) sushupti – prajna
(deep sleep state)

Brahman and Its Modes

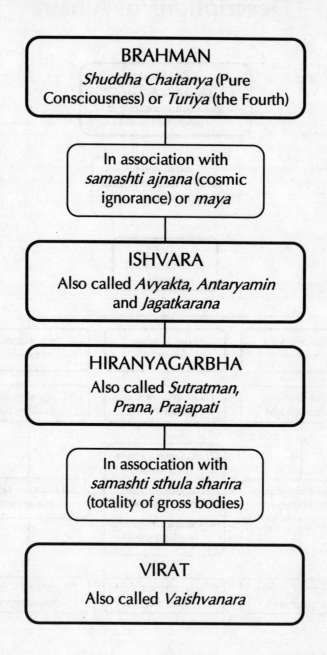

BRAHMAN

Shuddha Chaitanya (Pure Consciousness) or *Turiya* (the Fourth)

In association with *samashti ajnana* (cosmic ignorance) or *maya*

ISHVARA

Also called *Avyakta, Antaryamin* and *Jagatkarana*

HIRANYAGARBHA

Also called *Sutratman, Prana, Prajapati*

In association with *samashti sthula sharira* (totality of gross bodies)

VIRAT

Also called *Vaishvanara*

Descriptions of Ajnana

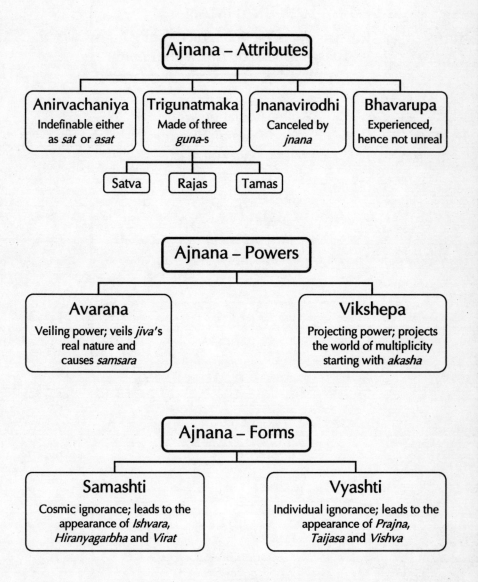

Ajnana – Attributes

Anirvachaniya
Indefinable either
as *sat* or *asat*

Trigunatmaka
Made of three
guna-s

Jnanavirodhi
Canceled by
jnana

Bhavarupa
Experienced,
hence not unreal

Satva Rajas Tamas

Ajnana – Powers

Avarana
Veiling power; veils *jiva*'s
real nature and
causes *samsara*

Vikshepa
Projecting power; projects
the world of multiplicity
starting with *akasha*

Ajnana – Forms

Samashti
Cosmic ignorance; leads to the
appearance of *Ishvara*,
Hiranyagarbha and *Virat*

Vyashti
Individual ignorance; leads to the
appearance of *Prajna*,
Taijasa and *Vishva*

Glossary

Glossary of Sanskrit Terms

ABHANAPADAKA – One of the two aspects of *avarana-shakti*. It hides the revelation of *Brahman*.

ABHASA – The false appearance of *Brahman* in *antahkarana* (internal organ).

ABHASA-VADA – The doctrine of false appearance. It explains the appearance of the individual soul (*jiva*) according to the *Varttika* School of Advaita.

ABHYASA – Repetition; one of the six characteristic signs (*shadvidha-linga*) used in determining the correct meaning of the great sentences (*mahavakya*-s).

ACHARYA – Teacher; preceptor

ACHINTYA-BHEDABHEDA – "Incomprehensible difference-nondifference". The theistic School of Vedanta founded by Chaitanya (1485-1533 AD.).

ADHYAROPA – Superimposition

ADHYASA – Superimposition due to delusion.

ADVAITA – "Non-dualism". The non-dualistic School of Vedanta founded by Shankara (c. 788-820 AD.).

ADVAITAM – Non-duality

ADVAYA – Non-dual

AGAMA – Verbal testimony; it is one of the six means of attaining valid knowledge (*pramana*-s) recognized in Advaita. It is also known as *sabda*.

AHAM BRAHMASMI – "I am *Brahman*". It is one of the four *mahavakya*-s or great sentences of the *Upanishad*-s and is found in *Yajur Veda, Brihadaranyaka Upanishad*, I.4.10.

AHAM-SPHURTI – An eternal expression of the Self. It is also called *vritti-jnana*.

AHAM-VRITTI – The activity of the ego. It is bound to lose itself and be replaced by *aham-sphurti*.

AJA – Birthless; unborn or non-created

AJATI – Birthlessness; non-origination or no-creation.

AJATI-VADA – The doctrine of non-origination or no-creation.

AJNANA – Ignorance; nescience

AKASHA – Ether; space

AMRITANUBHAVA – A short Advaitic work attributed to Jnanadeva (1275-1296 AD.).

ANADI – Beginningless

ANIRVACHANIYA – Indefinable; indeterminable

ANIRVACHANIYA-KHYATI –The theory of indefinable erroneous cognition.

ANTAHKARANA – The internal organ; it is constituted of mind (*manas*), intellect (*buddhi*), ego (*ahankara*) and memory (*chitta*).

ANUBHAVA – Intuitive realization of the Reality.

ANUMANA – Inference; it is one of the six means of attaining valid knowledge (*pramana*-s) recognized in Advaita.

ANUPALABDHI – Non-apprehension; it is one of the six means of attaining valid knowledge (*pramana*-s) recognized in Advaita.

ANUTPANNA – Un-originated

APAROKSHANUBHUTI – (1) Direct knowledge of the Absolute Reality. (2) A short treatise considered a standard work of Advaita. This text is attributed to Shankara and falls into the category of *prakarana grantha* (treatise on particular topics of philosophy).

APAURUSHEYA – Revealed but unauthored. It makes reference to the *Shruti*-s, considered unauthored texts.

APURVATA – Originality; one of the six characteristic signs (*shadvidha-linga*-s) used in determining the correct meaning of the great sentences (*mahavakya*-s).

ARAMBHA-VADA – Theory of creation according to which the effect is different from the cause. For example: a cloth being different from the thread, which composes it.

ARANYAKA – Text studied in the forest.

ARTHA – Worldly prosperity

ARTHAPATTI – Indirect inference; it is one of the six means of attaining valid knowledge (*pramana*-s) recognized in Advaita.

ARTHAVADA – Eulogy; one of the six characteristic signs (*shadvidha-linga*) used in determining the correct meaning of the great sentences (*mahavakya*-s).

ASANA – Body posture

ASAT – Non-existence; non-existent; unreality; unreal

ASATTVAPADAKA – One of the two aspects of *avarana-shakti*. It hides the existence of *Brahman*.

ASHTAVAKRA GITA – A brief treatise considered a standard work of Advaita consisting of 298 verses. This text is attributed to sage Ashtavakra and is also known as *Ashtavakra Samhita*.

ASTIKA – The group of orthodox philosophical systems (*Sankhya, Yoga, Nyaya, Vaisheshika, Mimamsa,* and *Vedanta*), which accept the authority of the *Veda*-s.

ATMABODHA – A very short treatise considered a standard work of Advaita. This text is attributed to Shankara and falls into the category of *prakarana grantha* (treatise on particular topics of philosophy).

ATMAN – The Self; identical with *Brahman*, the Absolute Reality.

ATYASHRAMI – Realized soul who is classed as beyond the four stages of life (*ashrama*-s) of Hindus.

AVACCHEDA-VADA – The doctrine of limitation; it explains the appearance of the individual soul (*jiva*) according to the *Bhamati* School of Advaita.

AVADHUTA GITA – A brief Advaitic treatise consisting of 193 verses. This text is attributed to sage Dattatreya.

AVARANA-SHAKTI – The veiling power of *avidya* or *ajnana* (ignorance). It veils the true nature of *Atman*.

AVASTHATRAYA-VIVEKA – Discrimination between the three states of waking, dreaming and deep sleep.

AVIDYA – Ignorance; nescience

AVIDYA-NIVRITTI – Cancellation of ignorance

AVYAKRITA – Undifferentiated

AVYAKTA – Unmanifested

AYAM ATMA BRAHMA – "This *Atman* is *Brahman*". It is one of the four *mahavakya*-s or great sentences of the *Upanishad*-s and is found in *Atharva Veda, Mandukya Upanishad,* 2.

BANDHA – Bondage; the state of the ignorant individual soul

BHAGAVAD GITA – "Song of the Lord". It is one of the greatest and most beautiful of the Hindu scriptures, containing 700 verses divided into 18 chapters, in quasi-dialogue form. It is the Book VI of the *Mahabharata*, "Great Epic of the Bharata Dynasty".

BHAGAVAN – The Lord of the universe; *Ishvara*. One who possesses all the six qualities called *Bhaga*: (1) *samagra* (all wealth of the world), (2) *dharma* (righteousness), (3) *yasa* (fame), (4) *sriya* (all success and prosperity in all directions), (5) *jnana* (knowledge), and (6) *vairagya* (dispassion and detachment). Great sages and saints are also often addressed as *Bhagavan* (e.g. Bhagavan Sri Ramana Maharshi).

BHAJA GOVINDAM – A very short poem attributed to Shankara.

BHAKTI – Devotion to God

BHAKTI-MARGA – The path of devotion

BHAMATI PRASTHANA – One of the three schools of Advaita, established by Vacaspati Misra (9th century AD).

BHASHYA – Commentary on ancient texts.

BHIKSHU – Renunciate; monk

BHOGA – Enjoyment

BHRAMASAMSKARA – Error impression

BIMBA – The original object

BRAHMA – God of the Hindu Trinity, considered the Creator of the Universe.

BRAHMA SATYAM JAGAT MITHYA JIVO BRAHMAIVA NA PARAH – One of the most famous statements of Shankara. It means: "*Brahman* is real, the universe is illusory and *jiva* is non-different from *Brahman*".

🕉

BRAHMA SUTRA – One of the principal texts of Vedanta. It is a great treatise containing 555 aphorisms and it is ascribed to Rishi Badarayana.

BRAHMA-BHAVA – To be as *Brahman*; to abide as *Brahman*

BRAHMAKARA-VRITTI – The mental modification in the form of *Brahman.*

BRAHMAN – The Absolute; the non-dual Reality

BRAHMANA – The caste of priests in Hindu society. A member of the priestly caste.

BRAHMANANDA – The bliss (*ananda*) of *Brahman*; it is the highest form of bliss.

BRAHMA-VIDYA – Knowledge or wisdom of *Brahman*

BUDDHA-DHARMA – One of the greatest religions and philosophical systems of the world. Founded by Siddhartha Gautama (5th century BC.) in northeast India, it spread throughout Asia.

BUDDHI – The intellect

CHARVAKA – Also called *Lokayata* (the view of the common people). A materialistic philosophical system that rejects the notion of an afterworld, the authority of the *Veda*-s, and the immortality of the self. It recognizes only direct perception (*anubhava*) as the means of knowledge (*pramana*). This philosophy was founded by Charvaka (c. 5th century BC.) and disappeared by the end of the medieval period.

CHINTAMANI – The Philosopher's Stone

DAKSHINAMURTI STOTRA – A very short work on Advaita. This text is attributed to Shankara and falls into the category of *prakarana grantha* (treatise on particular topics of philosophy).

DAMA – Control of senses; one of the six spiritual sub-disciplines (*samadi-shatka*) in Advaita.

DARSHANA – Philosophical system

DASANAMI – The order of monks (*Dasanami Sampradaya*) established by Shankara, where ten (*dasa*) names (*nama*) are added as suffixes to the names of the renunciates (*sannyasin*-s). These names are: *Sagara, Parvata, Giri, Puri, Bharati, Sarasvati, Tirtha, Ashrama, Vana* and *Aranya*.

DHARANA – The state of steady concentration

DHARMA – Basic nature, righteousness, performance of good actions and religious duty.

DHYANA – The state of meditation

DRIK-DRISHYA VIVEKA – Discrimination of the seer from the seen.

DRISHTI-SRISHTI VADA – The doctrine of simultaneous creation and perception of the world.

DUKHA – Suffering, sorrow, misery

DVAITA – "Dualism". The theistic School of Vedanta founded by Madhva (1199-1276 AD.).

DVAITADVAITA – "Dualism-nondualism". The theistic School of Vedanta founded by Nimbarka (c. 11th century AD.).

EKA-JIVA VADA – The doctrine that proclaims the existence of only one soul (*jiva*).

GURU – Master; teacher

GURU-PARAMPARA – Lineage of teachers

ICHCHA – The power of will

ISHVARA – The personal God or *Brahman* with attributes (*Saguna Brahman*). Primary, the three gods, *Brahma, Vishnu* and *Shiva* considered as one God. Secondary all other gods like *Durga, Lakshmi, Sarasvati, Ganesha*, etc.

ॐ

JADA – Grossness

JAGAT – The phenomenal world; the universe

JAGRAT – The waking state

JAINA – Jainism, a religion and philosophical system that rejects the authority of the *Veda*-s. This tradition refers to twenty four teachers (*tirthankara*-s or *jina*-s) of which the last one, Mahavira (c. 5th century BC.), was the founder. *Jain*-s do not believe in God, but in the divinity that dwells within every soul. Liberation is attained through right belief, knowledge, and action, whereby the practice of non-injury (*ahimsa*) of all living creatures is particularly stressed. The liberated souls are venerated as Supreme Spirits.

JANMADIVIKARARAHITA – "Devoid of changes or mutations like birth, growth, death, etc". It is a term which describes the nature of *Brahman* and *Atman*.

JATI – Birth; creation or origination

JIVA – The individual soul. Essentially it is the same as *Atman* (the individual Self) and Brahman, but has apparent limitations.

JIVAN-MUKTI – Liberation while alive. The liberation attained while still in the physical body.

JNANA – Knowledge; Self-knowledge

JNANA-KANDA – Portion of the *Veda*-s dealing with the knowledge of *Brahman*. It is contained in the *Upanishad*-s and differs from *karma-kanda* (the portion of rituals) contained by the *Samhita*-s, *Brahmana*-s.

JNANA-MARGA – The path of knowledge

JNANI – One who possesses Self-knowledge

KALA – Time

KALPITA-SAMVRITI – Imagined relative truth

KAMA – Desire

KARMA – Action or ritual.

KARMA-KANDA – Portion of the *Veda*-s dealing with rituals. It is contained in the *Samhita*-s, and *Brahmana*-s, and differs from *jnana-kanda* (the portion of knowledge) found in the *Upanishad*-s.

KARMA-MARGA – Path of action

KHYATI – Cognition

KOSHA – Sheath or covering. There are five sheaths that envelope the Self (*Atman*): (1) *annamaya-kosha* (food sheath), (2) *pranamaya kosha* (vital sheath), (3) *manomaya-kosha* (mental sheath), (4) *vijnanamaya-kosha* (intelligence sheath) and (5) *anandamaya-kosha* (bliss sheath).

KOTYA CHATASRA – The four statements that can be made when referred to a thing: "is", "is not", "is and is not" or "neither is nor is not". But none of these apply to *Brahman* or the Absolute Reality because It is beyond any definition.

KRIDA – Play; sport

KUMBHAKA – Holding the breath within

KUTASTHA – The immutable Self, the substratum of the universe

MAHABHARATA – "The Great Epic of the Bharata Dynasty"; one of the two great Hindu epics. It consists of 106,000 verses in eighteen books. Its author is ascribed to be Rishi Vyasa.

MAHAVAKYA – "Great Sentences"; they are used in transmitting the transcendental teaching concerning the identity between *jiva*, *Atman* and *Brahman*.

MALA – The prayer garland of beads consisting of 108 beads made of *rudraksha* seeds, lotus seeds, *tulsi* wood, sandalwood, etc.

ॐ

MANANA – Reflection; one of the three stages of practice in Advaita.

MANDUKYA KARIKA – The Advaitic treatise considered to mark the beginning of the systematized Advaita. This text is attributed to Gaudapada (c. 7-8th century AD.) and is an explanatory text on *Mandukya Upanishad.*

MATHA – Monastery

MAYA – Firstly it is defined as the illusive power (the cause of the phenomenal world) and secondly it is the phenomenal world itself (the effect).

MERU – The holy mountain in Hindu tradition representing the center of the universe.

MIMAMSA – It means "reflection" and is one of the nine Indian philosophical systems (*darshana*-s). Known also as *Purva-Mimamsa*, it is primarily concerned with the ritualistic acts found in the *Veda*-s. The principal text is *Mimamsa Sutra,* which was written by the founder of this philosophical system, Rishi Jaimini (c. 4th century BC.).

MITHYA-JNANA – Erroneous or false knowledge

MOKSHA – Liberation; the state of *Brahman*, attained by *jiva* (individual soul) simultaneous with the cancellation of ignorance (*avidya*).

MUKTA – A liberated soul. One who attained Self-knowledge or *Brahman.*

MULAVIDYA – Primal nescience; it is one of the two types of ignorance in Bhamati School. This is also known as *karanavidya.*

MUMUKSHUTVA – Desire for liberation

NAMA-RUPA – Name and form; the phenomenal world

NASTIKA – The group of heterodox philosophical systems (*Charvaka, Jaina* and *Buddha-Dharma*), which do not recognize the authority of the *Veda*-s.

NIDIDHYASANA – Deep meditation; one of the three stages of practice in Advaita

NIMITTA – The efficient cause of the world

NITYANITYA VASTU VIVEKA – Discrimination of the real from the non-real

NYAYA – Indian philosophical system of logic founded by Gotama (c. 6th - 3rd century BC.). It is also known as "*Tarkavidya*" or "science of logical proof" and offers a well-founded system for the inquiry into the objects and the subject of human knowledge. The main texts of *Nyaya* are *Nyaya Sutra* and *Tarka Sangraha*.

NYAYA-PRASTHANA – One of the principal texts of Vedanta; it is the name given to *Brahma Sutra*, a text on logic (*nyaya*).

OM – The most sacred syllable and symbol in Hinduism; It symbolizes Brahman and is also known as *AUM* or *Pranava*.

PANCHADASI – A treatise considered a standard work of Advaita. This text is attributed to Svami Vidyaranya (c. 1296 – 1386 AD.), who was one of the heads of *Shringheri Matha*, and falls into the category of *prakriya grantha* (treatise dealing with philosophical modes of operating).

PANCHAKOSHA VIVEKA – Discrimination of the five sheaths – which envelope and hide *Atman* – from the *Atman*.

PARAMAGURU – Grandteacher

PARAMARTHIKA-SATYA – The Absolute Reality or Truth; it is the non-dual *Brahman* and represents the Absolute and only final view of truth.

PARATANTRABHINISPATTI – The relative truth of the dependent apparent world.

PARINAMA VADA – The theory of real transformation. Type of material causality which involves real change or transformation, giving rise to real effects. For example the real transformation of milk gives rise to a real effect called curd. This theory is promoted in *Sankhya* philosophy.

PHALA – Fruit or result; one of the six characteristic signs (*shadvidha-linga*) used in determining the correct meaning of the great sentences (*mahavakya*-s).

PRAJNA – Consciousness

PRAJNANAM BRAHMA – "Consciousness is *Brahman*". It is one of the four *mahavakya*-s or great sentences of the *Upanishad*-s and is found in *Rig Veda, Aitareya Upanishad*, V.3.

PRAKRITI – Nature, matter. The primal matter of which the universe consists of.

PRAMA – Valid knowledge

PRAMANA – The means of attaining valid knowledge. Advaita recognizes six *pramana*-s: (1) perception (*pratyaksha*), (2) inference (*anumana*), (3) verbal testimony (*agama* or *sabda*), (4) analogy (*upamana*), (5) indirect inference (*arthapatti*) and (6) non-apprehension (*anupalabdhi*).

PRANA – The life or life-force of the universe.

PRANAVA – Term used to refer to the sound of the sacred syllable *OM*.

PRANAYAMA – Control of *prana* or control of breathing

PRAPANCHOPASHAMA – "Devoid of the world of multiplicity"; this statement makes reference to the non-dual nature of *Atman* and *Brahman*.

ॐ

PRARABDHA-KARMA – The actions done in past lives, which created and sustain the body in the actual life.

PRASTHANA – School of thought

PRASTHANATRAYA – The triple canon of Vedanta: (1) The *Upanishad*-s, (2) the *Brahma Sutra*, and (3) the *Bhagavad Gita*. The fundamental texts of Vedanta.

PRATIBHASIKA-SATYA – The illusory reality or truth; it is the false appearance of something where it does not really exist and represents only a preliminary and temporary view of truth.

PRATIBIMBA – The reflection of *Brahman* in *antahkarana* (internal organ).

PRATIBIMBA-VADA – The doctrine of reflection. It explains the appearance of the individual soul (*jiva*) according to the *Vivarana* School of Advaita.

PRATYAKSHA – Perception; it is one of the six means of attaining valid knowledge (*pramana*-s) recognized in Advaita. It is the most important of all six.

PURANA – Ancient mythological scriptures written in verse form, containing stories and legends of gods. The eighteen principal *purana*-s are often grouped according to whether they praise god *Vishnu*, *Shiva*, or *Brahma*.

PURNA – Full, plenary or complete. It defines the nature of *Brahman*, the Absolute.

PURUSHA – In general, it means spirit or Self; the *Atman* or *Brahman*.

RAJAS – One of the three tendencies or modes (*guna*-s) of nature (*prakriti*). It represents the mood of desire, action, and restlessness.

RIBHU GITA – An important work on Advaita. This text is part of the epic *Shivarahasya*, and contains the dialog between Sage Ribhu and his disciple Nidagha.

ॐ

RISHI – Term used to refer to seers, sages and poets. In Vedic tradition the Seven Great *Rishi*-s are those to whom the hymns of the *Veda*-s were revealed.

SABDA – Verbal testimony; it is one of the six means of attaining valid knowledge (*pramana*-s) recognized in Advaita. It is also known as *agama*.

SADAKA – Aspirant to liberation, seeker or one who follows a spiritual discipline.

SAD-ASAD-VILAKSHANA – Category of perceived objects, different from both the real (*sat*) and the unreal (*asat*).

SADHANA-CHATUSTAYA – The four prerequisite disciplines for enlightenment: (1) Discrimination (*viveka*), (2) renunciation (*vairagya*), (3) the group of six spiritual sub-disciplines (*samadi-shatka*) and (4) desire for liberation (*mumukshutva*).

SAMADHANA – Concentration of mind; one of the six spiritual sub-disciplines (*samadi-shatka*) in Advaita.

SAMADI-SHATKA – the group of six spiritual sub-disciplines: *shama* (tranquility of mind), *dama* (control of senses), *uparati* (cessation of senses), *titiksha* (forbearance of the pairs of opposites), *samadhana* (concentration of mind) and *shraddha* (faith in scriptural truths).

SAMHITA – The first section of each *Veda*. It contains the collections of Vedic hymns.

SAMPRADAYA – Lineage of spiritual teachers

SAMSARA – Cycle of birth, death and rebirth, to which every human being is subjected until ignorance is removed and liberation (*moksha*) attained.

SAMVRITI-SATYA – The empirical reality or truth; it is the world of "the born", or "the created". It is synonymous with *vyavaharika-satya*.

SANKALPA – Imagination, intention or will

SANKHYA – The Indian philosophical system founded by Kapila (c. 6th century BC?). *Sankhya* adopts a consistent dualism of the orders of matter (*prakriti*) and soul or self (*purusha*), and there is belief in an infinite number of similar but separate *purusha*-s, no one superior to the other. *Purusha* and *prakriti* being sufficient to explain the universe, the existence of a god is not hypothesized. The main text of *Sankhya* is *Sankhya Karika.*

SANNYASA – Renunciation; the fourth and final stage of life, when a Hindu renounces the world and directs his efforts toward liberation (*moksha*).

SANNYASIN – One who has renounced the world and lives solely for the attainment of liberation (*moksha*).

SARVAM KHALVIDAM BRAHMA – "All this is *Brahman* ". This statement is found in *Sama Veda, Chandogya Upanishad*, III.14.1.

SAT – The Absolute Existence; *Brahman*

SAT-CIT-ANANDA – Absolute Existence-Consciousness-Bliss; *Atman*'s three-in-one nature or essential form (*svarupalakshana*).

SATTVA – One of the three tendencies or modes (*guna*-s) of nature (*prakriti*). It represents the mood of spirituality, awareness, light and wisdom.

SATYA – The Truth; true or real

SATYAM JNANAM ANANTAM BRAHMA – "*Brahman* is Reality, Knowledge, Infinity". Famous statement describing the nature of *Brahman*, found in *Taittiriya Upanishad*, II. 1. 3.

SHADVIDHA-LINGA – The six characteristic signs used in determining the correct meaning of the great sentences (*mahavakya*-s): (1) Beginning and conclusion (*upakrama-upasamhara*, (2) originality (*apurvata*), (3) fruit or result (*phala*), (4) eulogy (*arthavada*), (5) *abhyasa* (repetition) and (6) reasoning or demonstration (*upapatti*).

🕉

SHAIVA – Shivaism; one of three major religious sects of Hinduism. The other two are *Vaishnava* and *Shakta*. *Shaiva*-s consider god *Shiva* as the Supreme Being and devote themselves to his worship. Two *Shaiva* schools are well known: *Shaiva Siddhanta* and *Shaiva Kashmira* (or *Pratyabhijna*).

SHAIVA KASHMIRA – The North Indian school of *Shaiva* sect; its philosophical doctrine is idealistic and monistic. This school is also called *Pratyabhijna*.

SHAIVA SIDDHANTA – The South Indian school of *Shaiva* sect; its philosophical doctrine is realistic and dualistic.

SHAKTI – Term which generally means power or energy. It is synonymous with *maya* and represents the creative power of *Brahman*.

SHAMA – Tranquility of the mind; one of the six spiritual sub-disciplines (*samadi-shatka*) in Advaita.

SHARIRA – Body, perishable form. Three bodies envelop the Self (*atman*): (1) *sthula-sharira* (gross body), (2) *sukshma-sharira* (subtle body) and (3) *karana-sharira* (causal body).

SHISHYA – Disciple; student

SHIVA – God of the Hindu Trinity, considered the Destroyer of the Universe.

SHRADDHA – Faith in scriptural truths; one of the six spiritual sub-disciplines (*samadi-shatka*) in Advaita.

SHRAVANA – Hearing; one of the three stages of practice in Advaita

SHRUTI – The "heard text" or "revealed text". The name of the *Veda*-s, the revealed scriptures of Hindus. The sacred texts belonging to this category do not have human authors.

SHRUTI-PRASTHANA – One of the principal texts of Vedanta; it is the name given to the *Upanishad*-s, revealed texts (*Shruti*-s).

SHUDDHA-CHAITANYA – The Pure Consciousness; the Self or *Brahman*

SHUDDHADVAITA – "Pure Advaita". The theistic School of Vedanta founded by Vallabha (1479-1531 AD.).

SHUNYA – Void or emptiness; it is one of the central concepts in Buddhism.

SIDDHASAN – The "perfect pose". Sitting posture used during meditation.

SMRITI – The "remembered text" or "recollected text"; the scriptures of Hindus coming after the *Shruti*-s (revealed texts). The sacred texts belonging to this category have human authors.

SMRITI-PRASTHANA – One of the principal texts of Vedanta; it is the name given to *Bhagavad Gita*, a *Smriti* (remembered text).

SO'HAM – "I am That". This is the mantra repeated through the sound made by the natural movement of the breath.

SRISHTI-DRISHTI-VADA – The doctrine of gradual creation and perception of it.

SUSHUPTI – The deep sleep state

SVAPNA – The dream state

SVARUPA – The innermost essence; the Self or one's own nature

TAIJASA – The dreaming state

TAMAS – One of the three tendencies or modes (*guna*-s) of nature (*prakriti*). It represents the mood of ignorance, inertia and laziness.

TARKA – Logic or reasoning

TAT TVAM ASI – "That you are". It is one of the *mahavakya*-s or great sentences of the *Upanishad*-s and is found in *Sama Veda, Chandogya Upanishad*, VI.8.7.

TILAKA – A mark, of ash or colored powder, made on the forehead and considered auspicious.

TITIKSHA – Forbearance of the pairs of opposites; one of the six spiritual sub-disciplines (*samadi-shatka*) in Advaita.

TULAVIDYA – Resultant nescience; it is one of the two types of ignorance in Bhamati School. This is also known as *karyavidya*.

TURIYA – "The Fourth" plane or the Self. The Reality transcending the three states (*avasthatraya*) of waking, dreaming and deep sleep.

UPADANA – Material cause

UPADESHA SAHASRI – A short treatise considered a standard work of Advaita. This text is attributed to Shankara and belongs to the category of *prakarana grantha* (treatise on particular topics of philosophy).

UPADHI – "Limiting adjunct". In Advaita this term refers to the names, forms, attributes and states taken up by the *Atman* when is identifying itself with the body, mind, senses, and ego. *Upadhi* refers to everything that is superimposed on *Brahman*.

UPAKRAMA-UPASAMHARA – Beginning and conclusion; one of the six characteristic signs (*shadvidha-linga*) used in determining the correct meaning of the great sentences (*mahavakya*-s).

UPAMANA – Analogy; one of the six means of attaining valid knowledge (*pramana*-s) recognized in Advaita.

UPANISHAD – The last sections of the *Veda*-s containing the philosophy or knowledge of Brahman. They are regarded as the most authoritative texts and are known as *jnana-kanda* (the portion of knowledge).

ॐ

UPAPATTI – Reasoning, demonstration; one of the six characteristic signs (*shadvidha-linga*) used in determining the correct meaning of the great sentences (*mahavakya*-s).

UPARATI – Cessation of senses; one of the six spiritual sub-disciplines (*samadi-shatka*) in Advaita.

VADA – Theory; doctrine or point of view

VAIRAGYA – Renunciation; one of the four prerequisite disciplines for enlightenment (*sadhana-chatustaya*).

VAISHESHIKA – Indian philosophical system founded by Kanada (c. 2nd – 4th century AD?). It lists six categories of real essences (*padartha*-s) and attempts to identify, inventory, and classify the real essences and their relationships as they present themselves to human perception. The main text of *Vaisheshika* is *Vaisheshika Sutra.*

VAISHNAVA – Vishnuism; one of three major religious sects of Hinduism. The other two are *Shaiva* and *Shakta*. *Vaishnava*-s consider god *Vishnu* as the Supreme Being and devote themselves to his worship. Two theistic and dualistic *Vaishnava* schools are well known: *Vishistadvaita Vedanta* and *Dvaita Vedanta*.

VAISHVANARA – The waking state

VARTTIKA – Type of work representing a critique on a philosophical commentary.

VARTTIKA PRASTHANA – One of the three schools of Advaita established by Sureshvara (8th century A.D.) and Sarvajnatma (8th century A.D.).

VASANANANDA – The bliss (*ananda*) that is left behind as impressions (*vasana*-s) of the highest form of bliss (*Brahmananda*).

VEDA – The most sacred texts of Hindu religion. They are called *Shruti* (heard texts), regarded as *apaurusheya* (revealed but unauthored texts), and have uncontested authority. There are four *Veda*-s and the first three are accepted by tradition as principal and most important: *Rig Veda*, *Yajur Veda*, *Sama Veda*, and *Atharva Veda*.

ॐ

VEDANTA – It means "Conclusion of the *Veda-s*" and is one of the nine Indian philosophical systems (*darshana*-s). Known also as *Uttara-Mimamsa*, it deals with the knowledge of *Atman* and *Brahman* as described in the *Upanishad*-s. Vedanta was founded by Rishi Badarayana (c. 5th century BC – 2nd century AD?) and has as principal texts a triple canon: (1) The *Upanishad*-s, (2) the *Brahma Sutra*, and (3) the *Bhagavad Gita*.

VIDEHA-MUKTI – Liberation after death. The type of liberation attained after the falling-off of the physical body.

VIKSHEPA-SHAKTI – The projecting power of *avidya* or *ajnana* (ignorance). It accounts for the appearance of the world and the individual souls by apparently transforming *Atman*.

VISHIAYANANDA – The bliss (*ananda*) resulting from the fulfillment of worldly desires and from the contact with the sense objects.

VISHISHTADVAITA – "Qualified-nondualism". The theistic School of Vedanta founded by Ramanuja (c. 1055-1137 AD.).

VISHNU – God of the Hindu Trinity, considered the Preserver of the Universe.

VIVARANA PRASTHANA – One of the three schools of Advaita, established by Padmapada (8th century A.D.) and Prakashatma (12th century A.D.).

VIVARTA-VADA – The theory of apparent transformation. Type of material causality which involves apparent change or transformation, giving rise to apparent effects. For example, the water of the ocean gives rise to waves and foam, which are essentially water and therefore considered only apparent transformations or effects of water. This theory is promoted in Advaita Vedanta philosophy.

VIVEKA – Discrimination; one of the four prerequisite disciplines for enlightenment (*sadhana-chatustaya*).

ॐ

VIVEKACHUDAMANI – "Crest Jewel of Discrimination"; a treatise considered a standard work of Advaita. This work is attributed to Shankara and belongs to the category of *prakarana grantha* (treatise on particular topics of philosophy).

VRITTI – Mental modification or mental wave. The mind consists of different *vritti*-s.

VRITTI-JNANA – The modal (*vritti*) consciousness or knowledge

VYAVAHARIKA-SATYA – The empirical reality or truth; it is the empirical world of names, forms and experiences and represents only a preliminary and temporary view of truth.

YOGA – The Indian philosophical system founded by Rishi Patanjali (*c.* 2nd century BC?). It is based on the *Sankhya* philosophy but differs by adopting the concept of *Ishvara*. Its influence has been widespread among many other systems of Indian thought. Its principal text is the *Yoga Sutra*.

YOGA VASISHTHA – A great Advaitic text attributed to Rishi Valmiki, in which Rishi Vasishtha teaches his pupil *Rama* about the nature of *Brahman*, the Absolute Reality and that of the phenomenal world. This work contains 32,000 verses.

VIVEKACHUDAMANI — ... One level of discrimination ... is also considered a standard work of Adwaita. This work is attributed to Shankara and belongs to the school (in prose and ...) treatise on part of the Gita of Bhishm).

PRITI — Mental modification (mental state) ... The mind confines to different points.

VRITTI-VYAYA — ...the modification, consciousness or knowledge ...

VYAVAHARA-SATYA — The empirical reality or truth. It is the empirical worldly sense ... personal experiences and represents ... by a preliminary and temporary view of truth.

YOGA — ... union philosophical system founded by Rishi Patanjali. The system offers as its basis of its standardised practices but differs by adopting the concept of Kaivalya. It has been widely used among many other systems of Indian thought. Its practice is called Yoga-Sutra.

YOGA-VASISTHA — A great Advaitic text attributes to Valmiki in which Rama is taught by Rishi Vasistha the Nature of Bondage, the Absolute Reality and that of the Phenomenal World. The work contains 32,000 verses.

Sources

Advaita Wisdom

– *The Upanishads*, (Vol. I, II, III, IV), (1975) ~ Swami Nikhilananda, Ramakrishna-Vivekananda Center, New York, USA.

– *Eight Upanishads*, (Vol. 1 & 2), (1998) ~ Swami Gambhirananda, Advaita Ashrama, Calcutta, India.

– *Brahma Sutra*, (2000) ~ Swami Gambhirananda, Advaita Ashrama, Calcutta, India.

– *The Bhagavad Gita*, (2001) ~ Alladi Mahadeva Sastry, Samata Books, Madras, India.

– *The Vision and the Way of Vasistha*, (1993) ~ Samvid, Indian Heritage Trust, Madras, India.

– *Astavakra Samhita*, (1998) ~ Swami Nityaswarupananda, Advaita Ashrama, Calcutta, India.

– *Ashtavakra Gita*, ~ John Richards, unpublished.

– *Mandukya Upanishad and the Agama Sastra*, (1992) ~ Thomas E. Woods, Motilal Banarsidass, Delhi, India.

ॐ

– *Ribhu Gita*, (1995) ~ Dr. H. Ramamoorthy & Master Nome, Society of Abidance in Truth, Santa Cruz, USA.

– *Avadhuta Gita*, (1994) ~ Swami Chetanananda, Advaita Ashrama, Calcutta, India.

– *Vivekacudamani*, ~ Swami Turiyananda, Sri Ramakrishna Math, Madras, India.

– *Upadesha Sahasri*, ~ Swami Jagadananda, Sri Ramakrishna Math, Madras, India.

– *Aparokshanubhuti*, (2001) ~ Swami Chinmayananda, Central Chinmaya Mission Trust, Mumbai, India.

– *Atmabodha*, ~ James B. Swartz, unpublished.

– *Dakshinamurti Stotra*, (2001) ~ Alladi Mahadeva Sastry, Samata Books, Madras, India.

– *Bhaja Govindam*, (1982) ~ Swami Chinmayananda, Central Chinmaya Mission Trust, Mumbai, India.

– *Amritanubhava*, (1997) ~ Ramchandra Keshav Bhagwat, Samata Books & Sri Mira Trust, Madras, India.

– *Pancadasi*, ~ Swami Swahananda, Sri Ramakrishna Math, Madras, India.

– *Sarva Gita Sara*, (1999) ~ Swami Sivananda, The Divine Life Society, Rishikesh, India.

Ramana Wisdom

– *The Collected Works of Sri Ramana Maharshi*, (2001) ~ Sri Ramanasramam, Tiruvannamalai, India.

– *Talks with Sri Ramana Maharshi*, (1996) ~ Sri Ramanasramam, Tiruvannamalai, India.

ॐ

– *Conscious Immortality*, (1998) ~ Sri Ramanasramam, Tiruvannamalai, India.

– *Be as You Are*, (1992) ~ David Godman, Penguin Books, New Delhi, India.

– *Absolute Consciousness*, ~ Grace J. Martin, Ramana Maharshi Centre for Learning, Bangalore, India.

– *A Practical Guide to Know Yourself*, ~ A. R. Natarajan, Ramana Maharshi Centre for Learning, Bangalore, India.

– *Jnana Marga in Bhagavan Ramana's Own Words*, ~ Sanjay Lohia, Ramana Maharshi Centre for Learning, Bangalore, India.

Zen Wisdom

– *Pearls of Zen and Tao Wisdom*, ~ Lee Chang, Unpublished.

– *Zen Speaks: Shouts of Nothingness*, (1994) ~ Tsai Chih Chung, Brian Bruya, Anchor Books, New York, USA.

– *Wisdom of the Zen Masters: The Quest for Enlightenment*, (1998) ~ Tsai Chih Chung, Brian Bruya, Anchor Books, New York, USA.

Tao Wisdom

– *Pearls of Zen and Tao Wisdom*, ~ Lee Chang, Unpublished.

– *The Tao Speaks: Lao Tzu's Whispers of Wisdom*, (1995) ~ Tsai Chih Chung, Brian Bruya, Anchor Books, New York, USA.

– *The Dao of Zhuangzi: The Harmony of Nature*, (1997) ~ Tsai Chih Chung, Brian Bruya, Anchor Books, New York, USA.